If your dog
could talk...

If your dog could talk...

Based on material from *Know Your Dog*

DR. BRUCE FOGLE

DK

LONDON, NEW YORK, MELBOURNE,
MUNICH, AND DELHI

DORLING KINDERSLEY
Project Editor Georgina Garner
Editorial Assistant Miezan van Zyl
Managing Editor Liz Wheeler
US Editor Christine Heilman
Managing Art Editor Philip Ormerod
DTP Designer John Goldsmid
Production Controllers Sarah Sherlock, Shane Higgins
Picture Researcher Louise Thomas
Publishing Director Jonathan Metcalf
Art Director Bryn Walls

PRODUCED FOR DORLING KINDERSLEY BY
SANDS PUBLISHING SOLUTIONS
Project Editors David & Sylvia Tombesi-Walton
Project Art Editor Simon Murrell

First American edition published in 1992, as *Know Your Dog*.
This fully revised American edition first published in 2006 by
DK Publishing, Inc.
375 Hudson Street
New York, New York 10014

06 07 08 09 10   10 9 8 7 6 5 4 3 2 1

A Cataloging-in-Publication record for this book
is available from the Library of Congress.

ISBN-13: 978-0-7566-1335-8
ISBN-10: 0-7566-1335-3

Reproduced in Singapore by Colourscan
Printed and bound in Singapore by Tien Wah Press

Discover more at
www.dk.com

Contents

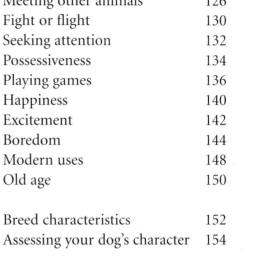

Foreword

"You're a dreadful dog owner," my wife tells me, hands on hips, exhibiting what I hope is just mock disdain. "All you do when you take Macy for her exercise is teach her bad manners!" Ouch! Julia's comment has a sting to it. She's hitting really close to the target: our mild-mannered, girly golden retriever regularly comes back from her exercise panting and exhausted, covered in mud from the tip of her gorgeous nose through to the end of her swishing tail. More often than not she smells like a million decomposing night crawlers. Macy thrives on her twice-daily liberation from household captivity. And on those early morning and late afternoon walks, she spends an hour or two just acting like a dog. When she slows down to a walk, there's a spring to her gait, as if she were gliding on a magic carpet.

Macy is a happy dog when she's outdoors—not because I've taught her bad manners but because, when we're out walking, I look at her pleading eyes and can't help but let her behave as her canine abilities compel her to. I think I understand what she's telling me she wants to do, and I simply let her do it. In that sense, let me say right now, before I go any farther, that if you want an obedient, responsive, and well-mannered dog, do as I say (in the following pages), not as I do.

A typical walk with Macy begins with a burst of frenetic exercise from her, a release of pent-up energy, followed by immediate attention to her bodily functions. After she's emptied both storage systems (and I've cleaned up after her), she raises her periscope and does one of two things: either she looks for other dogs to meet or she goes squirrel- and rabbit-hunting. When other dogs are present, because she is neither dominant nor submissive but rather, as the ideal dog is, "subdominant" (*see pp.74–75 for an explanation of subdominance*), she trots or gallops to the nearest dog, reading its body language as she goes. If the body language is not to her liking, she simply moves on, often to another dog.

When Macy reads appropriate body language from another canine, she greets it and picks up news by sniffing the dog's butt and, sometimes, its ears. She may instantly start playing or, if she's meeting a brand-new dog, play-bow first.

Just as often—more so recently—Macy decides to hunt instead. I call her the "squirrel police," enforcing the unwritten law that squirrels should always stay in trees. I try to make a joke of what she's doing, but to Macy this is no joke. Hunting is what she evolved to do to survive. She's faster than a squirrel and has learned their escape tactics, adapting her hunting techniques to match. Two years ago she first experienced success, and since then she's refined her hunting skills.

Because she's from one of the most trainable and controllable of all breeds, I can shout "Drop!" when she catches a squirrel or rabbit, and often she will. Yes, I know—I should have her under my control at all times. That's what Julia means when she says I'm ruining a well-mannered dog, but—and I find this hard to explain, even to myself—there's a tug within me that makes me want to let Macy fulfill her canine abilities.

As any spaniel or retriever owner knows, there are certain dogs that feel compelled to get wet. Even on the driest of days, if there's anything stagnant and disgusting that my dog can get herself into, she will. Dead fish or decomposing mammals and even fox droppings are, to Macy, the sweetest and most alluring of perfumes. She's an inveterate stick-chewer. Yes, I know the dangers there, too. As a practicing vet, I'm called upon to treat injuries that sticks cause in mouths and throats, and some of these are truly devastating. Even so, I let her chew, roll, meet potentially aggressive dogs, and bog-snorkel in the most repellent slime because, even after close to four decades of working with dogs, I'm still learning, and my own dog is as good a teacher as any I've ever lived with. In the following pages, I hope you enjoy seeing and reading about what dogs do and, through their actions and activities, establish a better understanding of what they are saying to other dogs—and, of course, that means to us, too.

DR. BRUCE FOGLE

Introduction

ANYONE WHO HAS SPENT even a little time with dogs knows how attuned they become to their human environment. Of all the species that have ever lived with humans, the dog has adapted best to a human landscape. This is a species with an uncanny ability to understand what we want. But are we anywhere near as good at understanding what dogs want?

Canis familiaris, the member of the canine family with which we are most familiar, certainly shares common behaviors with us humans. We are both gregarious species that enjoy—indeed, thrive on—the companionship of others of our own kind. We both have a natural inclination to live within packs in which there is a defined hierarchy. We work well with others and are most content either with an acknowledged leader to respect and follow, or when we become leaders ourselves. Humans and canines share a range of feelings and emotions: we can be affectionate, jealous, envious, tolerant, giving, selfish, vulnerable, content, angry, or upset with others. Our needs are so similar that the dog was the first animal to be invited into our homes and, eventually, our hearts. It's a cliché but it's true: throughout the world, over the centuries, the dog has become "man's best friend."

LONG-TERM RELATIONSHIP

All dogs descend from a line of Asian wolves that adapted long ago to living near humans. While archaeological evidence confirms that this relationship is at least 15,000 years old, genetic evidence suggests that the original adaptation might

Wolf in dog's clothing
Despite the myriad different guises in which today's dogs can be found, they are all essentially "new," "improved" versions of the wolf.

have occurred long before—perhaps 45,000 or more years ago. Whatever the time scale, there is little doubt that dogs accompanied our ancestors from their nomadic wanderings and temporary camp sites to fixed settlements and villages, and then on to urban centers, where most of today's 400 million dogs now live. They made these transitions so successfully because they are highly skilled at adapting to rapidly changing conditions. My own dog has the good fortune to spend weekends outdoors, ground-trailing in the woods or beach-combing on the seashore. Then, when work beckons me back to the city, she is equally adapted to play activity with other dogs or humans, or simply lounging on the carpet. Within the canine species there is the potential for the most dramatic range of shapes and sizes, and this has helped in its transition from wolf to wolf-dog to dog, but it is its varied

nature that has made the dog the most popular animal companion there has ever been.

MODERNIZING THE DOG

Primitive dogs carried the genetic potential for a wide range of different characteristics to help them survive in varying environments. With a little help from us, those characteristics were accentuated through selective breeding, creating the hundreds of breeds that exist today. Genetic evidence shows that, while there are more than 400 recognized breeds today, few are truly ancient. The vast majority of them were created through our intervention in the last 200 to 300 years.

Most breeds exist today at our whim. We create new breeds—the Labradoodle is an example—or lose old ones—for instance, the Tweed spaniel, the progenitor of the modern golden retriever—according to our needs or wants. Because of this,

some scientists have avoided studying the dog, arguing that it is an unnatural, even warped, product of human intervention. More recently, science has realized that a unique opportunity to study genetic adaptation has been afforded by the genetic adaptation of the wolf into the great variety of dog breeds that now exist. Through this we can better understand how individual or groups of genes control physical characteristics, behaviors, and, perhaps most important, predisposition to disease.

Virtually all dog breeds have been developed out of artificial rather than natural selection. Even the Australian dingo and the Papua New Guinea singing dog, which until recently mated without the pressure of human selection, are based on our intervention, because thousands of years ago humans introduced "domesticated" dogs to these regions. All of our canine companions today are the result of the practical, aesthetic, economic, nutritional, or even ritual needs of preceding human generations. Some dogs are more independent, while others have been bred to become more trainable or obedient.

THE DOG'S "INTELLIGENCE"

It is easy to confuse what suits us best in a dog's behavior with what is naturally best for the dog itself, thinking that the more trainable a dog is, the more intelligent it is. In fact, the independent feral dog that survives on its wits might be more naturally "intelligent" than the dog that jumps through hoops on command. The word "intelligence" is so fraught with misconceptions that I am going to avoid it in this book. Instead, I will discuss learning abilities. Dogs have a variety of learning centers in their brains and, through selective breeding, we have augmented some and diminished others. Whichever way you look at it, "domestication" has reduced the volume of the dog's brain to 75 percent of that of its wolf ancestor. In spite of all our interventions, the wolf ancestry remains overwhelmingly evident in our dogs. Over

Emergency rations
These chow chows are descendants of guard dogs bred in China. Their ancestors would also have been a source of food in times of famine.

A dog of two halves
This Labradoodle, produced by intentionally crossing a Labrador retriever with a standard poodle, has been bred solely for its role as a family companion.

Ability to learn
More than any other species studied, including primates, the dog is adept at understanding human "intention movements," what we want it to do. This Belgian shepherd reads its trainer's demand to sit.

Blending in
The long-haired Briard resembles the sheep it was bred to protect, the likeness acting as a camouflage to fool wolf predators.

99.8 percent of their genes are shared. Even in those breeds that are the most dramatically different, the bedrock of their original behavior survives. They think like pack animals, use their senses like pack animals, behave with their own kind and with us like pack animals. The dog has the senses of the hunter. It courts, mates, and raises its young in the same way as the wolf. It communicates with us as a member of a wolf pack communicates with other pack members. Some breeds are more "wolf" than others in their communication, but all are wholly wolf in the core of their behaviors.

Because we share so many needs, emotions, and patterns of behavior with dogs, and because we have been influencing their characters for thousands of years, it is easier for us to understand what dogs are trying to tell us than it is to understand any other domesticated species. Most of us live in surprisingly close contact with our dogs. We share our homes and, often, our cars, furniture, and bedrooms with them. Surveys in North America and Europe consistently reveal that more than half of our dogs sleep in our bedrooms, often on our beds.

DIFFERENCES BETWEEN HUMANS AND DOGS

Dogs have become so integrated into our families that it is easy to forget that they differ from us in many ways. It is easy to misinterpret what they are trying to tell us. My clients frequently tell me that their dog did something to "get even." Humans get even; dogs don't. Dogs chew and mess out of anxiety or boredom, not revenge.

In order to understand your dog, it is vital to understand that, just as we often think of our dogs as humans in strange disguises, they think of us as rather odd dogs. We might be bigger than them, we certainly smell different, and we are able to do awesome things like drive cars to the park or open cans of food, but they still only think of us as other dogs and communicate with us accordingly. Their relationships with us are wholly based on this immutable fact. To the core of its being, even the smallest and fluffiest dog will always remain true to its roots: a wolf in disguise.

1 WHAT IS A DOG?

The dog is a human invention. While its ancestor, the Asian wolf, chose to live in close proximity to humans, the modern dog, perhaps the most adaptable ever of all land-based carnivores, survives at our whim. A key element behind this adaptation is that dogs appear to understand what we want and, equally, we seem to understand what they want.

While archaeological records show that our relationship with dogs has existed for almost 15,000 years, genetic studies of dogs suggest that our cohabitation dates back much farther. Indeed, the fact that the people who migrated across the Bering land bridge 14,000 years ago brought their dogs with them certainly suggests a mutually beneficial relationship was already well established.

There is little doubt that your dog descends from a small group of Asian wolves. Geneticists can now identify the breed of a dog simply by examining genetic material collected on a cheek swab, and they have been able to create a genetic family tree for canines. A few breeds are known to be truly ancient, but the great majority of the world's 400 or so breeds have been "created" by us over the last 200 to 300 years, mostly in Europe but also in North America.

We have created these breeds because the dog remains useful to us even though, for most of us, its utilitarian function is now negligible. Even those who still work their dogs do so for pleasure rather

One of a crowd
Although their appearances and temperaments vary, all dogs—like their ancestor, the Asian wolf—are pack animals, needing social contact in order to thrive.

than to find food, defend themselves, or to use them for transportation. During the 20th century, the dog's role changed. Today, our canine buddies provide us with often indefinable gains that are more social and psychological than functional. We get rewards from our dogs because, through their body language and their behavior, they talk to us in ways we enjoy listening to. We maintain a steady level of dog ownership because the dog has a phenomenally elastic ability to adapt and evolve to meet our needs. And, increasingly, dogs are bred and trained for new roles, becoming members of the human family.

Modern genetics has revealed where dogs come from, and new techniques in genetic manipulation may, if used benignly, accelerate the dog's natural evolution. It is equally possible that modern science may be corrupted to create a new dog species with a superabundance of the values we now desire.

We are not the first to wonder exactly what a dog is. Nor is our relationship with dogs really that new. More than 2,700 years ago, in what is now Iran, the Persian Zoroastrians had a perfect understanding of dogs. In their holy book, the Zend Avesta, the dog was described as having the patience of the priest, the protectiveness and ferocity of the warrior, the willingness to work the long hours of the livestock farmer, the joy of the strolling singer, the fondness of the night of the thief, the shamelessness of the wild beast, and the faithlessness of the courtesan, yet the tenderness of the child. I don't know about you, but that certainly describes my dog.

The dog evolves

GENETIC EVIDENCE indicates that your dog is a modified wolf, and the first modification from wolf to dog took place in east Asia between 15,000 and 100,000 years ago. At some time in the distant past, three more genetic modifications took place, creating the groundwork for the variety of breeds we have today.

Until 1997, some scientists believed certain dogs were descended from jackals. In that year, an international team of scientists published the results of research into wolves, jackals, coyotes, and dogs. They studied genetic material called mitochondrial DNA.

Mitochondria are structures within cells, the DNA of which comes entirely from the mother. The line of descent is female to female. Over time, mutations are inevitable. The mutations produce diverging lines of mitochondrial DNA, but they remain constant, giving a unique signature to a line of descent.

IT'S IN THE GENES

The scientists learned that *all* dogs share their mitochondrial DNA with wolves. There is a direct line of descent. None shared its mitochondrial DNA with jackals or coyotes. Further investigation revealed that three out of four modern dogs share their mitochondrial DNA with a single female wolf ancestor. In other words, three quarters of all dogs today descend from one family of wolves. The remaining one in four shares its mitochondrial DNA with three other wolf ancestors. This means that there was probably one defining genetic event in which the wolf adapted to a life in cohabitation with humans and became the "dog."

Later on, but still in ancient times, other wolves mated with these "dogs" on three other occasions, leading to the three minor lines of descent.

Dog and wolf similarities
Anatomically, both dogs and wolves are built to chase, capture, kill, and eat meat. Socially and psychologically, they are adapted to live with others, using gestures and body language to defuse potential conflict.

VARIETY OF WOLVES

Today, when we think of wolves, we usually think of majestic North American timber-wolf packs or of the more independent European gray wolf. But there are many "breeds" of wolf that once existed or still exist today. In North America alone there were once more than 20 different wolf breeds. Some were massive—up to 135 lb (60 kg) in weight—and have been hunted to extinction within the last 100 years. In Asia, wolves were much smaller, with the Japanese wolf, or shamanu, about the size of a springer spaniel.

The wolves that dogs evolved from have also evolved, but you can readily see the ancestry of the Asian pariah dogs in the Asian and Indian wolves and the Nordic spitz breeds in the European and North American wolves. Evolution can occur surprisingly swiftly, and by 12,000 years ago, the ancestors of all modern breeds already existed.

European gray wolf
Only a few European gray wolves survive today, living in the most remote, mountainous regions of Europe. This wolf augments breeding stock from which some local dogs evolved.

Asian wolf
The Asian wolves, smaller than their European and North American cousins, are the probable source of the original wolf-dogs, individuals that chose to live close to human habitations.

Prehistoric canines, ancestors of wolves, evolved in North America and spread to Eurasia

Modern canines evolved in Asia and spread to North America

North American timber wolf
Long before Europeans reached the Americas, Asian migrants brought their dogs with them. These crossed with indigenous wolves, creating local breeds.

Indian wolf
Having spread throughout Arabia and into Africa, the Indian wolf may have passed its genes on to dog breeds as diverse as the basenji, saluki, Pekingese, and dingo.

The dog's domestication

IT SEEMS REASONABLE TO ASSUME that primitive dogs, physically identical to wolves, formed a loose, scavenging association with ancient humans. However, this is only an assumption, since their fossils cannot be differentiated from wolf fossils. There are certainly wolf bones found with human fossils dating back tens of thousands of years, but were these wolves prey or primitive companions?

In parts of Asia, and even in Europe, archaeological sites predating the development of agriculture have yielded recognizable dog bones alongside human bones. Researchers at the British Museum have confirmed that a jaw bone found in a cave in Iraq occupied by people 14,000 years ago was that of an equally ancient domesticated dog. Israeli archaeologists discovered a 12,500-year-old human grave in which a dog pup was held in a seemingly warm embrace by its female owner. In Spain, an even older burial site was excavated, revealing the skeleton of a girl. Around the girl, facing in four directions, were four dogs. Firm archaeological evidence reveals that humans and "proto-dogs" (primitive dogs) had formed a relationship well before our ancestors settled into permanent agricultural sites.

CHANGING LIFESTYLES

When our ancestors became agricultural and first settled into permanent villages, the wolf-dog came under new, unique pressures, and this is when its shape dramatically changed, leaving the first extensive fossil evidence of the modern dog: a smaller brain cavity, more compacted teeth, a smaller body. Within a short time, the shape of the dog evolved enormously. Archaeological evidence, as well as bas-relief carvings, show that sight hounds, ancestors of the modern Afghan, saluki, and greyhound, existed in Mesopotamia 6,000–7,000 years ago. More than 5,000 years ago, guarding dogs, ancestors of Rottweilers and bulldogs, existed in Tibet; small-eared, densely coated Nordic dogs, ancestors of the modern spitzes, existed in Siberia and northern Europe; while miniature dogs, ancestors of the pug, the Pekingese, and the Maltese, existed in China and Egypt.

Cave paintings
This cave painting, found in the Algerian Sahara and dating from 4000–1500 BC, shows that, even then, dogs resembling today's pariah dogs assisted man while hunting, perhaps by following scent.

Ancient myth

In the western Mexican state of Colima, a pre-Columbian myth describes dogs as the guardians of the underworld. This terra-cotta dog figurine dates from *c.* 200 BC–300 AD.

Islamic imagery

This 17th-century painting shows the comic character Mullah Dopiaza seated on an emaciated horse. The dog is typical of both the pariah dogs and sight hounds common at that time.

Pottery and bas-reliefs show that herding dogs, not unlike the modern Canaan dog, were used in Israel around 4,200 years ago. By 3,200 years ago, short-legged herding dogs existed as far away as Wales. Paintings and tapestries show that scent hounds, their bodies covered in short thin hair suited to warm weather, the ancestors of the modern basset hound and dachshund, were evident in Italy 1,700 years ago. Water spaniels and retrievers made their appearance in Europe 1,300 years ago, and terriers only 100 years later. Throughout the world, the dog's relationship with us was varied and evolving— and getting ever closer.

Early hunters

This Greek amphora, thought to date from the late 6th century BC, clearly shows a dog accompanying men on a hunt.

The word "dog"

Before genetic evidence confirmed that all dogs have a single geographic origin, there were already linguistic clues to the species' origins. Throughout the world, most of the words we use to specify "dog" have common roots in ancient languages. Look at this list.

- ancient Chinese   k'iuon
- ancient Japanese   ken
- Indo-European   k'uon
- ancient Greek   kyon
- Latin   canis
- Italian   cane
- Romanian   canac
- old Spanish   can
- French   chien
- East African   kunano

In some languages, the Indo-European "k" evolved, or "sound-shifted," to "h." *Kuon* became *huon*, and so the Dutch *hond*, German and Scandinavian *hund*, and English "hound."

In other languages, *kuon* sound-shifted to *shuon*, evolving to the Sanskrit *shvan* and Armenian *shun*.

From east Asia, through the Middle East to Europe and Africa, as the dog migrated, so did the original word used to describe it.

Learning centers in the brain

DOGS HAVE BEEN BRED for many utilitarian reasons: to guard, attack, herd, chase, fight, kill, follow scent trails, point, set, retrieve, pull carts and sleds, turn spits, and simply to comfort. They are capable of such varied tasks because their minds are flexible. They inherited from the wolf a selection of hardwired biological "learning centers" in their brains, related to abilities the wolf needed to survive and breed. Through selective breeding, we have enhanced some of these learning centers and diminished others.

One of the factors that differentiate a dog's learning capabilities from ours is the influence of culture. In humans, behavior spreads from person to person; this is the basis of our religious beliefs, our fashion sense, even our food preferences. Not so in the dog.

Dogs read us like books

Here is a simple test that scientists carried out. They hid food under one of two containers (designed so that no food odor escaped from the container), then let chimps, wolves, and young and adult dogs select which container had the food. They gave some clues by gazing at the right container, by pointing at it, or by tapping on it. Dogs and pups quickly "got it"; wolves and chimps did not. Somehow, in the evolution of the dog's brain, the species improved its ability to read us, to take cues from humans that adult wolves or chimpanzees are not capable of recognizing.

Other than in puppyhood, dogs are relatively poor learners from the "culture" of other dogs. In that sense, there are limited cultural influences on their behavior. Your dog's ability to think and to communicate with you is based on the array of abilities it inherited from the wolf.

Cerebrum

Thalamus gland

Reticular formation

Pineal gland

Pituitary

Hypothalamus

Cerebellum

Midbrain

Brain stem

Spinal cord

The brain
All sensory information is converted into chemical messages for transmission and analysis by the brain. Some messages influence the pineal gland, in the base of the brain, which synchronizes all body rhythms.

Sentinel duties
Investigation—while patrolling their territory, for example—is one activity for which dogs have learning centers.

Understanding mating
How to mate, when, and with whom are key learning-center elements, as is the initial sexual attraction.

Self-preservation
Left to their own devices, dogs are extremely good at finding safe places to live, where they will feel protected.

IDENTIFYING LEARNING CENTERS

Among others, I believe dogs have learning centers for the following abilities:

- The value of relationships, both dominance and kinship: "I'll let my pup do that to me, but I won't let anyone else."
- The need and ability to mate: "I know who is who and which end is which."
- A knowledge of motion and forces; understanding mechanics: "That branch is going to fall on me."
- A capacity to map large territories mentally: "I can find my way home."
- Choosing where to live, both for safety and for productivity: "Under that table looks perfect for me."

- The intuition to patrol, investigate, and mark territory: "I need to check out what passed this way yesterday."
- An understanding of danger and how to be cautious: "Is it safe to walk that narrow path?"
- An ability to know what should and should not be eaten: "I'll eat these berries but not the leaves."
- An understanding of the behavior of other animals, including predicting their behavior from their actions: "I'll chase the small one but not the big one."

EFFICIENCY OF "WIRING"

All dogs inherit hardwired modules for these specific types of behavior, but in some breeds, modules for certain behaviors are more efficiently wired than for others. That is why Yorkshire terriers are picky eaters, while Labradors eat anything, and why dachshunds bark when they are looked at, but beagles do not seem to notice even a dominant stare. When you try to understand what your dog is telling you, remember: its abilities to learn and communicate are those of the wolf. Your canine friend is not just a human in disguise.

Interpersonal essentials
Dogs have innate knowledge of certain things, including those vital to the furtherance of the species. These include understanding their relationships with those around them and their role within the relationships.

Breed evolution

THE GREATEST GENETIC DIVERSITY among dogs exists in east Asia, and this is the strongest evidence for their geographical origins. Genetic research, studying what scientists call microsatellite DNA data, has explored this diversity. Microsatellites are snippets of DNA with known locations on the chromosome. Microsatellite DNA sequences are shared among closely related individuals. Geneticists studied 85 dog breeds and observed that they all fit into one of four different clusters of related breeds (*see right*). Of these four clusters, three have relatively recent origins, evolving within the last 200–300 years. This indicates to us that most breeds of dog are, in fact, modern. The dogs in these three categories appear to have been bred for use by humans in guarding, hunting, and herding.

WHAT IS DOMESTICATION?

Pet dogs are "domesticated" in the sense that they have successfully acclimatized to life on our terms. But what makes them so willing to do so?

An answer to this question comes from fascinating studies of another canine—the fox. In Britain over the last 20 years, the fox has successfully acclimatized to living in a densely populated human environment, and its "flight distance"—how likely it is to flee when being approached by something unfamiliar—has diminished.

In a selective-breeding program, within just ten generations, Russian biologist Dimitri Belyaev "domesticated" the red fox. He produced individuals that sought out human companionship, barked more, and often had drooping lop ears. In effect, he perpetuated the cub in the fox. He produced individuals that were lifelong juveniles. That is exactly what we did with dogs, and it is what we treasure in their personalities. Dogs are forever youthful, always curious, and reliably responsive to their human "parents."

Dog-breed clusters

The four clusters into which the 85 studied breeds fell are shown here. One cluster of breeds, those with the widest diversity of traits, is the most primitive, and the dogs in this group are genetically the closest descendants of the first Asian wolf-dogs. These are found in List 1.

The remaining lists are altogether more modern. The second list comprises the genetically oldest of these modern breeds and contains what could be called the guarding dogs, suggesting that this was once the most valued of canine abilities. A more recent group includes dogs with, generally speaking, herding behaviors (see List 3). The fourth list includes dogs with hunting behaviors.

What is instantly noticeable is that dogs that have similar looks do not necessarily belong in the same groups—for example, the boxer and Saint Bernard.

List 2: Guarding breeds

- Mastiff
- Bull mastiff
- Bulldog
- Miniature bulldog
- French bulldog
- Boxer
- Rottweiler
- Newfoundland
- Bernese mountain dog
- Perro de Presa Canario
- German shepherd

Boxer

German shepherd

List 1: The most primitive breeds

- Chow chow (China)
- Shar-Pei (China)
- Akita (Japan)
- Shiba Inu (Japan)
- Basenji (Africa)
- Siberian husky (northeast Siberia)
- Alaskan malamute
  (northwest Alaska)

Samoyed

Almost equally old, but not quite as ancient, are:

- Afghan hound (Afghanistan)
- Lhasa apso (Tibet)
- Pekingese (China)
- Saluki (Middle East)
- Samoyed (western Siberia)
- Shih Tzu (Tibet)
- Tibetan terrier (Tibet)

Siberian husky

List 3: Herding breeds

- Shetland sheepdog
- Belgian sheepdog
- Belgian Tervuren
- Collies
- Saint Bernard
- Old English sheepdog
- Irish wolfhound
- Greyhound
- Whippet
- Borzoi

Saint Bernard

List 4: Hunting breeds

- Golden retriever
- Labrador retriever
- Cocker spaniel
- Irish setter
- Basset hound
- Beagle
- Pointer
- Bloodhound
- Cairn terrier

- Airedale terrier
- Other spaniels, pointers,
  retrievers, terriers, and
  scent hounds

Irish setter

Beagle

"Intelligence" and "trainability"

I HEAR IT EVERY DAY: "Isn't she the most intelligent dog you've ever seen?", or "This it the most intelligent dog I've ever had." I read about it as well. I doubt there is a breed standard anywhere in the world that does not use the word "intelligent" in its description of that breed. But what does this word mean? And, just as importantly, what does its corollary "dumb" mean?

I am going to avoid using the word "intelligent," but it is still useful to try to understand what people mean when they use it. In essence, there are four different types of intelligence that we should think about when considering what our dogs are doing. These are skills and abilities that help a dog adapt to its environment, or alter its environment to make it better to live in.

LEARNING ABILITY

Generally speaking, dogs with good learning ability need only a few exposures to a situation in order to form stable responses. A perfect example is knowing exactly which cupboard their toys are kept in and coming running when it is opened.

PROBLEM-SOLVING

Slightly different is the skill of problem-solving; the faster a dog solves a problem, with the fewest false starts, the better its problem-solving capacity. For example, if you place a food reward on the far side of a barrier and attach it to a string running under the barrier and to the side where the dog is, how long does it take the dog to understand that if it pulls on the string, it gets the reward? Generally speaking, and certainly compared to primates, dogs are not that good at mental problem-solving, but some are better than others. Sheep-herding breeds such as the Border collie have been selectively bred for their problem-solving capabilities.

COMMUNICATION INTELLIGENCE

Sometimes called obedience intelligence or working intelligence, communication intelligence is what helps the dog work with humans. A dog may have good problem-solving and learning abilities, but it also needs

Learned or trained
This Border collie, following commands from the shepherd but also thinking for itself, exemplifies all aspects of canine intelligence: an ability to learn quickly, a facility for problem-solving, and an aptitude for understanding our commands.

efficient communication skills to understand what we want it to do. It needs a willingness to take directions and not be distracted. Dogs with longer attention spans and persistence are more capable of concentrating on a task. While learning ability and problem-solving help the dog act for itself, communication intelligence helps the dog interact with us.

INSTINCTIVE INTELLIGENCE

These are the forms of intelligence that are hardwired into the brain's various learning centers. Through selective breeding, we enhanced some dogs' inherited aptitudes and diminished others. Terriers are persistent diggers; toy dogs bark territorially; hounds howl to communicate; and retrievers retrieve.

Ranking communication intelligence

Psychologist Stanley Coren asked dog experts to rank breeds by their willingness to work and obey, according to their communication intelligence. The dogs with the poorest communication intelligence are the genetically oldest breeds, while those with the best communication intelligence have been developed since 1800.

The "most intelligent" were:

1. Border collie
2. Poodle
3. German shepherd
4. Golden retriever
5. Doberman
6. Shetland sheepdog
7. Labrador retriever

The "dumbest" were:

1. Afghan hound
2. Basenji
3. Bulldog
4. Chow chow
5. Borzoi
6. Bloodhound
7. Pekingese

Border collie is at the head of its class

Afghan: officially dumbest breed

2 STARTING A FAMILY

Few people ever have the chance to observe very early puppy behavior. It is only dog breeders who, on a daily basis, have the opportunity to watch a pup rapidly evolve—from its total dependence on its mother, to its willingness and confidence, only weeks later, to leave the pack and embark on a new life with a non-canine pack, moving into our homes.

The dog's success as a species is intimately connected to its willingness both to associate with humans and to be controlled by us. Nevertheless, there are occasions in a dog's life when its actions and behavior are wholly influenced by its biology, and this is at its most obvious during mating, pregnancy, and early puppy development. The almost perfunctory courtship and then curiously protracted physical linking during mating are the same for a tiny Chihuahua as a powerful Mastiff. So, too, is the behavior of the pregnant female: she becomes quieter, grows more possessive of articles such as toys, prefers to stay under tables or chairs, and sometimes becomes irritable, even snappy. These hormonally triggered changes also occur during the "false pregnancies" that follow each and every heat cycle.

At birth, the mother is in total control, instinctively severing the umbilical cords, licking the pups dry, and helping them find her milk. The pups themselves are born with only a few active senses and are completely dependent on her. But the pups' exquisite sensory abilities develop rapidly, within only a few weeks, and

Family history
A great advantage of acquiring your dog from a breeder is that it will give you a chance to see that the parents are healthy.

with them comes independence. Soon the pups are exploring their world, learning to manipulate both each other and any objects that they find, and demanding solid food as well as milk from their increasingly harassed mother.

While we speak of dogs as pack animals, this is the only time in the lives of most dogs that they are part of a wholly canine pack. The mother is, of course, pack leader, but a hierarchy soon develops within the litter, with the most dominant pups claiming the most productive nipples. A dog's personality is grounded in the early relationships it develops with its mother and littermates. Both dominant and submissive characteristics form early, long before you acquire your pup, and begin to influence the pup's emotional development.

Because we control their breeding, we can accentuate or diminish common behavioral characteristics shared by dogs. This is how we have successfully created a huge variety of breeds with differing temperaments. Some of these breeds are easily trained, while others are more independent; certain breeds thrive on human companionship, while others are very protective of their territories; some breeds are placid, and others more excitable. By choosing carefully, you can select a canine companion to enhance the lives of both you and your family.

Diverse personalities
All pups have different characteristics. When choosing a family pet, many people make a decision based on whether a pup is playful or quiet.

Topsy-turvy
These six-week-old puppies play rough-and-tumble, improving their coordination, balance, and reflexes.

Choosing a partner

ALTHOUGH IT MAY APPEAR that the male initiates courtship, it is actually the female who decides when—and with whom—she will mate. As she comes into season, over 10 to 14 days she increasingly urine-marks (*see pp.80–81*), leaving a scent trail for males to follow. She does not necessarily choose the most dominant male for mating. Females prefer familiar partners but, although they may bark and snap at overexcited suitors, they might simply roll over to overdominant dogs. While males are year-round sexually active "opportunists," females have only two short spells each year when they ovulate and mate. Just before, during, and after ovulation, bitches become more flirtatious and playful, soliciting interest from male dogs.

The female cycle

A female dog reaches sexual maturity as early as five months of age, long before emotional maturity. The first sign of the onset of her reproductive cycle is a visible swelling of her vulva, followed a day later by a bloody discharge. She may also behave in a more skittish manner. This initial phase, called "proestrus," lasts 4–15 days (though typically 10–12), after which the discharge stops, eggs are released, and the female is receptive, for 4–8 days, to mating. Typically, the cycle occurs twice yearly, but once a year or three times a year are not uncommon.

1 Play-bowing
Having scented that the female is in season, the male dog confidently approaches her. She replies with a play-bow, which invites him to join in play activity while telling him that she is not yet ready to mate.

Bitch moves into play-bow stance

"Shouldn't I be doing that?!"

Dog pants heavily to cool off

Front paws surround dog's midriff

2 Role reversal
During pre-mating games, the female clasps the male from behind and mounts him. Sometimes she will also carry out pelvic thrusts. Although he is disconcerted, the male remains passive because of the prospect of mating.

3 Brief interlude
Standing still, with his tail wagging with excitement, the male allows the female to investigate him. She licks her nose to allow scent molecules to be caught more readily so she can scent him better. After a pause, play continues.

"Well, hello there, little lady!"

Ears pricked back in alert position

"Not so fast, buster—let's play first."

"Okay, I'm ready when you are."

4 Playing around
Play-wrestling is often initiated by the female. It allows her to make frequent body contact with her partner. Both dogs roll and tumble, growling all the time, while the male takes the opportunity to thrust with his pelvis.

5 Standing ready
Once she is certain that the male is an acceptable mate, the female stands still. She then draws her tail to the side, displaying her vulva. She will only behave in this way after ovulation.

Mating

AFTER THE SNIFFING, play-bowing, prancing, and dancing of courtship, the act of mating is completed fairly quickly. As soon as the bitch is ready for him, the dog mounts her, grasping her body with his forelegs. Experienced stud dogs have no problems with sexual union, but inexperienced males often need a little guidance. Help is best left to experienced dog breeders or veterinary staff. Occasionally, a male may gently hold on to the female with his teeth, to maintain his balance and grasp. Generally speaking, the male ejaculates quickly. Even so, the two dogs remain physically locked together in a "tie," often for more than half an hour. The tie, caused by part of the dog's penis, the bulbourethral gland, swelling after mating, temporarily prevents other dogs from mating with the female.

1 Standing receptively
As the female stands waiting with her tail turned to one side, the male excitedly sniffs and licks her vulva. If she resumes play, he will mark a nearby spot with urine. However, if she remains still, he knows that she is ready to mate.

Male sniffs and licks female's genital area

"I'm just waiting for you to say yes."

Tail is moved to one side, allowing access to genitals

Dog rests head on bitch's back

"I'm ready for you now."

Forelegs clasp female's body

"This will just take a minute."

2 Check and mate
Knowing the female is ready to mate, the male moves closer to her. Initially, he stands squarely to her side and rests his head on her back. He licks or nibbles her and, if she seems amenable, prepares to mount.

3 Copulation
While the bitch stands still to accommodate him, often with her eyes partly closed, the male clasps her waist with his forelegs. Next, he starts making pelvic thrusts. Ejaculation begins almost immediately.

4 The tie that binds
After mating, a balloonlike structure at the base of the dog's penis swells up, preventing the pair from separating. They remain locked together for up to 50 minutes. Once the dog's swelling subsides, the pair "untie" and retire to lick clean their genitals, reducing the chance of infection.

Dog closes his eyes and begins to relax

Pregnancy behavior

THE HORMONAL CHANGES OF PREGNANCY always follow ovulation, so it is very difficult to determine whether a bitch is pregnant or simply experiencing a perfectly normal "false pregnancy." Whether pregnancy occurs or not, the bitch becomes calmer and less active, and her abdomen begins to enlarge visibly. She may be inclined to spend more time alone, especially under furniture, to sleep more, and to carry her toys around with her. But pregnancy cannot be confirmed until the abdomen can be scanned or the pups manually felt in the womb three weeks later. When a female is genuinely pregnant, experienced breeders notice that her nipples begin to enlarge and freshen to a more vivid pink a few weeks after successful mating.

Toy possession
Finding security under a chair, a female dog exhibits her maternal behavior by caring for a stuffed toy, sniffing its ears and then licking them. She behaves this way after her season, regardless of whether or not she is really pregnant.

Phantom pregnancy

After eggs have been released from a female dog's ovaries, progesterone, the hormone that prepares the uterus for pregnancy, is spontaneously produced in the ovaries. This happens regardless of whether or not the released eggs were fertilized and the dog is truly pregnant. Progesterone production continues for two months after each ovulation and, if a bitch is not pregnant, causes a "false," or "phantom," pregnancy. During a false pregnancy, a bitch may experience taste-bud changes, temperament change, and milk production. In some individuals, the hormonal activity can be so similar to a true pregnancy that, at the end of her false pregnancy, the bitch loses her appetite and shows signs of experiencing mild contractions. In most instances, a phantom pregnancy is of no medical concern, but for some females, milk production becomes so uncomfortably excessive and mood changes so dramatic that veterinary intervention is beneficial. Before any treatment is administered, however, blood tests and a physical examination can confirm whether the problem is a phantom pregnancy or an unplanned true one.

Late pregnancy
In the last stage of pregnancy, this bitch lies on her side in what is now the most comfortable position for her. The size of her swollen abdomen indicates that she is due to give birth imminently.

Abdomen is distended by growing puppies

"What a weight to carry around."

"I have to find somebody to care for."

Mothering another species
Impelled by her need to nurture, this bitch has adopted a litter of orphaned kittens, which she grooms as she would her own puppies. Her behavior derives from both her past experience as a mother and the presence of progesterone.

Kittens investigate foster mother

Giving birth

THE CONTRACTIONS OF BIRTH are precipitated by an abrupt reduction in the levels of the pregnancy hormone progesterone and a coordinated increase in the production of estrogen. As this begins, some females become restless and stop eating. In some cases, they may be wary of strangers or even act aggressively if disturbed. Others, however, seek out their human owners and want them near. The intensity of the contractions of labor varies, and a bitch may groan, pant heavily, or take slow, deep breaths. Some dogs will temporarily inhibit their contractions when they see their owners. The first pup is usually delivered within a maximum of two hours of the onset of contractions, but usually sooner. Subsequent pups arrive after intervals ranging from a few minutes to two hours in length. Birth can be a difficult procedure in breeds with relatively large heads, such as the bulldog, or in breeds with small litters and consequently large pups, such as the Yorkshire terrier. If your dog experiences any difficulties, contact your vet immediately.

"Let's get you guys cleaned up."

1 Last things first
With rhythmic contractions, the mother expels a puppy in its birth sac. Most puppies emerge head first, in a diving position, but this one is coming tail first. The puppies that have already been born stay close to Mom for warmth.

2 Severing the ties
This experienced mother has already licked away the sac from the puppy's face, allowing it to breathe. She now turns her attention to chewing through the umbilical cord, severing the puppy from its afterbirth.

3 Licked into shape
The mother dries her puppies with meticulous licking and stimulates them to empty their bladders and bowels by licking the anogenital regions. These systems are already functioning but are not under the newborn puppies' control.

4 Mother's milk
By now, the mother has already eaten the pups' afterbirths, and she turns to check on the newborns' feeding arrangement. She is happy to let her puppies find her nipples as soon as they can.

*Puppies huddle
together for warmth
and to feed*

⑤ Well-earned rest
Having successfully delivered all six
puppies, licked them dry, and cleaned up
as much of the mess of birth as she can
to protect them from predators that may
smell them, the mother now relaxes and
gives her newborn family an uninterrupted
feeding. If undisturbed, she will not
leave her puppies for the next 24 hours.

*Eyes and ears are
closed at birth*

*"Hey, you're
not my
mommy!"*

⑥ Dependent offspring
Dry and with full stomachs, these
one-hour-old puppies are almost totally
helpless and completely dependent upon
their mother for warmth, food, and
protection. She will retrieve straying
puppies only if they cry out, but she
feeds them without their asking.

Good mothering

EVEN THE MOST HUMAN-ORIENTED DOG retains her natural mothering instinct, which is triggered by giving birth and the appearance and erratic movements of her puppies—the same factors that evoke caring instincts in humans. The mother's instinctive behavior progresses naturally from the initial total concern for her puppies' protection, nourishment, cleanliness, and sanitation, through the stage of teaching discipline while still putting up with her litter's shenanigans, and eventually to treating her young as other adult members of a pack when they represent competition for her. This rapidly evolving maternal behavior allows the pups to become independent from their mother by three months of age.

Teaching manners
Because she has been bitten too hard during play, the mother disciplines this puppy by pinning it to the ground. This teaches the pup to control the severity of its bites during play sessions.

Potty training
The mother stimulates one of her pups to urinate and defecate; she will continue to do this until the pups are three to four weeks old. To hide signs of the presence of her young from potential predators, she consumes their wastes.

"I'm a mom, but I can still have fun."

Game for anything
By joining in with her puppies' games, this mother helps them develop their coordination and reflexes. Play situations such as this often end in overt mothering activities, such as grooming.

Constant care

While two of her puppies feed, this experienced mother licks clean the ear of another. Feeding and grooming are pleasurable activities for her, but both become an increasing strain as the puppies mature and become more active.

"Who says you can't do two jobs at once?"

This three-week-old puppy can now feed standing up

Puppy love
Touch is perhaps the most underestimated of all senses.
Contact with its mother calms the pup: its heart rate falls
and it feels safe. The mother, too, is relaxed and at ease.
This physical bond is the basis for successful rearing of
young and the reason why adult dogs enjoy our touch.

Developing senses

AT BIRTH, THE ONLY EFFICIENT SENSES pups have are heat and scent receptors on and in their noses, and touch receptors on their bodies. These senses guide the newborns to find nourishment from their mother's nipples and to huddle together for warmth. A puppy's eyes and ears do not function until it is two weeks of age but subsequently develop quickly and are fully functional within another two weeks. Taste and smell, present at birth, also develop swiftly over the first five weeks of life. These senses provide pups with the necessary abilities for early independence. Early in life, a hungry pup cries for its mother. By three weeks of age, its senses—for example, the touch receptors on its feet—are so sophisticated that it can orient itself and seek out its mother for the nourishment it needs.

Defenseless pup remains still

Sight and sound
Although she has grown rapidly since birth, this one-week-old puppy remains deaf and sightless. In another week, her ears will open, and loud sounds will startle her.

Body heat
In the absence of their mother, these one-week-old puppies stay warm by huddling together.

"Mmm... so cozy and warm."

"Just taking a sniff."

Pup discovers source of scent

Precocious nose
A five-week-old puppy pauses in play to sniff the urine scent on his littermate. The scenting ability is present at birth and is mature by four weeks of age.

Pup begins to make small movements

Present and almost correct
They have been open for five days, but this two-week-old puppy's eyes are only now becoming functional. It will be another two weeks before the ability to see is developed.

Sleeping with you

Give your dog the option, and he or she will probably choose to sleep not just in the same room as you, but on your bed—probably in contact with you. Many dog owners look upon this preference as a canine act of love, but the likelihood is that, first and foremost, it fulfills some of the dog's own basic needs.

• Dogs want to sleep with us because the sense of touch is the most primitive—and perhaps the most powerful—of all senses.

• Immediately after birth, it is touch and warmth that draw the pup to its mother's nipple.

• Your dog's most basic feelings of security and contentment are perpetuated when it sleeps beside your body.

Comfort can be found even in uncomfortable-looking positions

"Do you mind if I lick you here?"

Puppy licks and sniffs ear

Someone to lean on
This five-week-old puppy sniffs at its mother's ear, balancing itself by placing a forepaw on her face. By the time it has reached this age, all of the pup's sensory abilities have already matured to adult level.

Licking and begging

FOR THE FIRST THREE WEEKS of life, it is Mom who decides when the pups will feed: she gains contentment from suckling her young, and she also responds to their vocal demands for her presence. As soon as they can walk, however, the pups start demanding food from her. Taking the initiative, they follow her around and try to feed whenever possible—even when she is simply standing still or eating her own meal. This behavior not only satisfies their hunger, but also acts as a family bonding mechanism. As the puppies' digestive systems mature, they eat their first solid foods. In the same way in which a mother wolf regurgitates solid food for her young after a hunt, some dogs do the same for their maturing puppies.

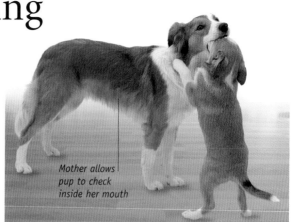

Mother allows pup to check inside her mouth

Recycled food
Sticking its muzzle into Mom's mouth, this puppy tries to stimulate her to regurgitate a meal. This is a way in which some dogs feed their young, and it is also why dogs willingly eat food that has just been vomited up.

A kiss before starving

All of us are familiar with the dog's natural inclination to greet us with a "kiss." You arrive home, and your dog wants to give you a lick—a face lick. If you're really honest with yourself, you know that your dog actually wants a mouth lick and is a closet French kisser. This is simply a natural evolution of the pup asking its returning mother for a meal. What your dog truly wants, though it might not even know it, is for you to regurgitate a treat.

Adapting natural behavior
While her mind is still completely open to learning, this Boston terrier puppy learns to beg for food from a human, her new "mother." She stands on her hind legs to get close to the food, just as she would to get near her mother's mouth.

Family provider
The puppies gather around their mother, pestering her for solid food. In the absence of human providers, she would now be bringing back meat from hunting for them to eat.

Old habits die hard
Seeing their chance, these six-week-old puppies latch on for a meal. Because feeding is also comforting to Mom, she stops what she is doing and permits them to suckle, even though they are now old enough to do without milk.

"I actually enjoy this a lot."

Learning to move

ALTHOUGH A PUPPY is virtually helpless at birth, its senses develop so rapidly that by a mere 12 weeks of age it has all the basic abilities necessary for its life. It can keep up with adults, avoid predators, and it understands the basic moves for capturing prey. All of this is possible simply because a puppy's nervous system matures so rapidly—incomparably quicker than the 18 years it takes for the human nervous system to complete its physical development. A pup can stand unaided just two weeks after birth, walk by three weeks of age, and run by five weeks. By 12 weeks of age it will have developed all the gaits of adulthood—the walk, trot, canter, and gallop. In addition to this, within the same time scale it will also have mastered the abilities needed for successful hunting: leaping, creeping, jumping, and crawling.

1 Three hours old
At birth, this puppy can right himself if he rolls over and can raise his head. Using heat sensors in his nose, he can also locate his mother and waddle to her.

"I feel so heavy…"

2 One week old
Although he has more thrusting power in his hind legs, there have been no dramatic changes in the puppy's mobility during the first seven days.

3 Two weeks old
Using all four legs, the puppy can now just raise himself off the ground. Improved coordination and balance allow him to take his first steps.

"Left… right… left…"

4 Three weeks old
The puppy can now make decisions about where he wants to be and is able to move in the direction of his choice.

Eyes are open
and focused

Puppy is now
much more steady
on his feet

"Wow! This
is amazing."

5 Six weeks old
The puppy has developed
dexterity and confidence in his
movements. His reflexes are well
developed and, combined with his
now mature senses, give him all the
skills he needs to investigate the
world around him.

Front paws can now be
placed with conviction
in direction of travel

Curiosity

ONCE THEIR SENSES and coordination are developed, puppies begin exploring their surroundings and their relationships with each other. They soon learn how to survive in and benefit from the world around them. They must also learn how to live with other members of their pack. At first, a pup's curiosity knows no fear or trepidation: he boldly leaves the nest and explores the surrounding territory, willingly approaching all animals, including us. This is a sensitive period in a pup's early life, and it will form the backbone of lifelong behavior. Although fear behavior begins to develop at seven to eight weeks of age (the age of the pups shown here), this important period of social exploration and open learning continues for about another month.

"There's something in my way."

"Now, that looks interesting."

2 Overcoming obstacles
In fact, the puppy's curiosity has been stimulated by something else. Too young to have learned that he could be encountering a serious fight and putting himself at risk, the puppy takes the shortest possible route to his destination, nonchalantly climbing over the other two puppies.

1 Off to explore
Seeing two of his littermates involved in physical activity, a third puppy appears to become interested in their behavior and approaches them.

"You seem twice as heavy now."

③ Straight ahead

Although they are being used as a jungle gym, the two littermates continue their spirited encounter. The inquisitive puppy is too interested in what he sees ahead to join in their activity and continues moving toward the focus of his attention.

④ Activity continues

As the lone puppy goes off to explore what intrigues him, his two littermates continue their play fight. The more the pups explore their surroundings and learn about each other at this age, the better prepared they will be for their adult lives.

Puppy gently bites playmate's neck

Hind leg stretches to climb over obstacle

Puppy goes on playing as though nothing has happened

"Up, over, and away."

What's new here?
The curiosity of youth is enchanting to watch, but it is also powerfully important for the emotional development of the dog. The more a pup experiences early in life, the more prepared it is later on. Dogs raised in stimulating environments have a head start in their adult lives.

Experiencing life

THE MOST INFLUENTIAL TIME in a pup's life is from birth until it is approximately three months old. For the first two-thirds of this period, pups are usually still with their mothers and living with their breeders, not under our control. This is when a pup learns how to act and react with other pups, and how to experience and use the world around it. Through trial and error, it discovers what is enjoyable and what is dangerous, what is edible and what is not, and what feels good and what is uncomfortable. Skills are honed. Mental and physical dexterity develops through play. The more a young dog is allowed to investigate its surroundings, the more developed—and, in fact, the heavier—its brain becomes.

Perils of the human world
Yarn provides a chewable feel that this Border collie puppy finds pleasurable. However, yarn can cause severe damage to a dog's intestines, so such play should be supervised—or stopped.

Is it edible?
Showing his excitement, this puppy play-bows while chewing on a toy. The chemical senses of smell and taste are the ones used first by puppies to investigate their surroundings.

"Keep your paws off – this is mine."

Sibling rivalry
Three littermates argue over who gets the prize. It seems appealing because they are fighting over a toy, but they would do the same over a recent kill.

"This tastes like nothing. Is it food?"

Good muscle
control has
developed

Puppy shows
good balance

Raised tail
shows interest

*"I wonder
if it will run
away."*

Checking it out
With a foreleg raised and extended,
this puppy examines a new object by
touching it. The pup will bat it around
for a while before tasting it.

Teething and chewing

Puppies taste life. It is perfectly natural—absolutely normal—for a pup to mouth anything: carpets, table legs, door frames, shoes, even you. Just because it is natural, however, it does not mean that it should be considered acceptable. Ensure that your pup has an outlet for its natural need to chew by providing it with safe and satisfying items to play with. Make sure these toys are completely different from other items your dog might find to chew. For example, do not give your pup an old shoe: he or she will not be able to differentiate between the old one and your very best new ones. You may think that a pup's chewing is at its worst at 8–18 weeks of age, when its

milk teeth are needle-sharp, but a pup's ability to cause serious damage begins in earnest after adult teeth have erupted. This is when a pup tries to discover exactly what its new set of powerful teeth is capable of. This is when maximum damage occurs, so make sure you provide satisfying outlets for this normal canine need.

Puppy play

DOGS REMAIN PLAYFUL throughout their lives, and this a characteristic of humans, too. It is for this reason that we have exaggerated the dog's joy of play through selective breeding—so much so that, in many ways, we have created what are, in essence, lifelong puppies. We enjoy watching them play, and we enjoy playing with them. Dogs are most playful when young, and through play they learn how to communicate with each other and, most importantly, how to inhibit their bite. Play stimulates inventiveness and teaches problem-solving, timing, balance, and coordination. It also allows puppies to experiment under safe conditions. Play often begins with a bow and ends abruptly when a pup gets distracted or bored.

Chewing you

Your pup will play with you just as it does with its littermates, and that means with its mouth. Often pups aim for the face, since this is where they get food from Mom. You must make it clear to your pup that no biting will be tolerated.

- When your pup bites in play, be theatrical, scream "ouch," and leave the room. Return a few seconds later, but avoid eye contact.

- By mimicking a littermate, you teach your pup that there are limits to vigorous play activity.

Formal bow
Asking to play, this puppy lowers itself into the classic play-bow position. Dogs use this stance to tell one another that they are not threatening and would simply like to meet. As an adult, this puppy will behave in the same way with humans or any other animals to which it has formed attachments.

"Will you play with me, please?"

"Don't do that again!"

Head is turned
in submission

Assertiveness training

Having been bitten too hard by a larger littermate, the smaller puppy bites back, warning that it will not be intimidated. The social ranking of puppies is determined in exchanges such as this.

Pup "attacks"
littermate

Chasing tails

These three littermates bite and chase each other. If they bite too hard, they will receive the same from their playmates in response, so they soon learn to bite gently.

"Fun, fun, fun! I'll take you both on!"

Tail is raised
in excitement

Face to face

Growling and facing each other, these pups are gently trying to bite each other's faces. This play activity will continue throughout their lives and is very common in adult dogs.

Lowered body
signifies submission

The extended family

IT IS A CURIOUS FACT that the only time in your dog's life during which it experiences true pack activity is the short period between its birth and its acquisition by you. Once a pup leaves its mother and siblings, it develops modified pack behavior, with your human family taking the place of other canine pack members. Only pups that go on to live or work with other dogs—pack hounds, for example—find themselves in a situation where they make their own decisions on the admission of new canine members to their group. Introducing a new dog into a home with an existing dog is, ultimately, always successful because of the inherent naturalness of the action. How that extension of the family develops depends on the age, sex, size, and self-confidence of the new pack member.

Order of seniority
Meeting these older dogs for the first time, this eight-week-old puppy is put in its place by a senior dog's confident show of authority.

"We all know each other really well."

Not one of us
Seeing a small stranger, a 12-week-old member of the pack intimidates it by dominantly placing a paw on the intruder's shoulder. The smaller outsider feels threatened by this action and soon backs away.

Integrating with others

When bringing a new pup into your home, allow your existing household companion to make the first moves. Keep the new pup in a closed room until it is deeply asleep, then let your resident do the initial investigating. Mature dogs are easily annoyed by the rambunctious, uninhibited glee of young pups, so it is wise to supervise early encounters, solely to be sure the older dog does not use excessive force.

"We don't like strangers around here."

"I used to be the boss of this pack."

Family saga
When possible, previous generations will continue to live with their litter. Older dogs are still members of the pack—in this case, the grandmother, her daughter from a previous litter, and the grown puppies—but as they age, they pass the leadership on to the next generation.

3 WHAT DOGS DO

Dogs are gregariously sociable. They thrive in the company of their own kind, but they are also able to fit in with the company of that equally sociable species, humans. Both dogs and humans share a common pack mentality of hunting, resting, eating, and sleeping together. Working together is what has made both such successful species.

The dog's pack mentality comes from its wolf forebears. After the last ice age, wolf packs radiated out throughout the Northern Hemisphere, following the herds of large hoofed animals that were their prey. We humans did the same, making us the only other social carnivore to migrate north at that time. Young wolves were probably captured, raised, and played with by our ancestors. It is likely, though, that

most would later have been eaten. However, the "tamest" individuals probably escaped this fate and would have been allowed to breed.

As in the wild, superior size and mental acuity decided who would lead in the packs of those dogs that evolved as a result of our intervention in breeding. But so did the dog's ability to follow the directions humans gave them through hand movements, facial expressions, or verbal instruction. Males usually dominate a pack because of their physical strength, but serious fighting is usually avoided. Instead, ritual threats, such as showing the teeth, lowering the head, staring, and growling, are used to maintain discipline and rank within the pack. Dogs learn these rituals and settle into a suitable position in the pack during play as

Non-blood ties
Pack dogs, such as these beagles, learn to live together and get along well with one another, despite originally coming from different families.

Afternoon snooze
Dogs like a good nap just as much as the next animal, spending up to half of each day napping. Only 20 percent of this is deep sleep.

young pups. Rough-and-tumble is fun in itself, but as pups mature play becomes rougher, leading to disputes that are won by the strongest in body and spirit.

Eventually the most dominant dog emerges, asserting authority through his body language. Most other pack members are usually content to submit to their leader—this is indicated through gestures and facial expressions—but eventually a spirited younger male will challenge the pack leader's authority.

Many other behavior patterns we see in our canine buddies are also remnants of this wolf-pack mentality. A canine pack needs a territory in which to hunt and rest. It marks out this territory with body wastes, especially urine, or sometimes with visible markers, made by kicking up earth after defecating.

The pack defends its territory, preventing others who are not pack members, be they dogs or humans, from entering it. Of course, even the most humanized dogs still hunt. Their predatory instinct makes fair game of anything that moves—from a mouse, to a squirrel, to a tennis ball, to a passing car.

Ultimately, the dog's unique ability—the superior ability that separates it from all other species, including primates— is its "social intelligence": its ability to understand and follow our instructions.

Building blocks
Canine littermates play-fight with one another in order to build their strength. Skills learned at this stage will serve them well later in life.

Natural talent
It takes very little training for dogs to become experts at catching balls— just like this German short-haired pointer—combining rapid reactions, eyesight, and hind-leg strength.

Coordinating activity

WITHIN THE DOG'S WOLF ANCESTORS, pack instinct evolved to help them capture prey larger than themselves. To be successful in the hunt, wolves must coordinate their activities, alerting each other to surrounding scents, sights, and sounds. This is what some behaviorists call "social intelligence," the dog's trump card in its evolution to the role of humankind's most loved animal companion. Cooperation is the most powerful aspect of the dog's behavioral repertoire and is one of the reasons why they make such good partners. Dogs coordinate their activities not only with each other, but also with our schedules. They sleep and wake to our timetables, run, chase, and play together, eat collectively, and join together when greeting us, our visitors, and other canine friends.

Working as a team

Sleeping together gives the members of a wolf pack mutual security and warmth. They all arise equally fit to work as a team. Once awakened, wolves become alert to a scent, sight, or sound and turn toward it. When one pack member finds a scent or hears a noise, his body language alerts the others. By coordinating their activities and working together, they are more alert to danger and better equipped to capture animals larger than themselves than they would be alone.

Dinner party
This pack of beagles eats and drinks communally from one bowl. They all know each other well, so there is no competition over who eats first.

Mother love
These long-haired dachshunds look up expectantly at their owner, hoping for food or attention. They respond as they did to their mother when they were puppies. Now, as adults, they coordinate their behavior with the activities of their human leader.

Outnumbered
Although they are far smaller than this Rhodesian ridgeback, these dominant Chihuahuas, who know each other and form a pack of two, eat first. The larger outsider simply stands by and watches.

"Awww, I love my mom."

Leg is raised in anticipation

Pack members stay close together

Teamwork

WHEN GIVEN THE OPPORTUNITY, many dogs readily follow the pack instinct that they have inherited from wolves and act as a team. The most dominant dog plays "team captain," and the rest willingly obey his command. The difference between a team of huskies and a wolf pack is that the huskies have two team captains: the top dog and the human pack leader. True pack behavior occurs only in dogs that have lived together for a sufficiently long time to form stable relationships. Stray dogs may join together fleetingly—for example, in following the scent of a female in season—but they do not coordinate their activity as closely as a true team does.

"You are the top dog really."

Owner shouts instructions from behind

Paying homage to the leader
The top dog in the husky pack leaps up to greet the real team leader. In all our relationships with dogs, the human must play the part of "top dog."

Pulling together
The huskies follow the instructions shouted by their owner and surge ahead. They concentrate on working as a team and are eager to start running as soon as they feel the harness.

The myth of the pack

While some wolves hunt for food cooperatively and exhibit true "pack-hunter" behavior, it is not an altogether common canine trait. As all sociable species do, groups of dogs develop a hierarchical structure in which the dominant individual makes decisions and the rest follow. That is the basis of our relationship with dogs and what we choose to call "teamwork": we decide and they participate. Pack-hunting behavior is not universal even in wolves. It may be normal in Canadian timber wolves but has never been so in European wolves. Coyotes, on the other hand, will hunt as a pack on occasions. The dog's mind, adapted to the niche of living with us, has evolved in its own direction.

"I used to do this as a puppy."

Relaxing together
The team relaxes as a group, a habit that started when, as puppies, they would huddle with their littermates for warmth. Although these dogs are not littermates, they have learned to behave as such with each other.

"Wait your turn—this one's mine."

Taking the cake
The pack leader leaps into the air to catch a tidbit thrown to the pack, while the rest of the team holds back. She has been chosen as leader by her owner, but the decision was influenced by her natural authority over the other dogs.

Tail is raised in excitement

"You lead and I'll follow."

A combined show of strength
Dogs have enduring stamina and naturally follow their pack leaders. Here, the top dog and his consort share leadership while the rest of the pack adds their strength, pulling a sled through the barren Arctic. Pulling on a leash is a natural dog behavior, essential for survival in the Far North.

Male and female behavior

THE PERENNIAL QUESTION of nature versus nurture applies to dogs as much as it does to humans. This much is known: from just before birth until a few days after, the male pup's testicles temporarily produce the male sex hormone testosterone. This hormone travels via the bloodstream throughout the body, including to the brain, where it is taken up by some nerve cells. It is a fair comment that male pups are "masculine" at birth, while female pups remain hormonally neutral until the female sex hormone estrogen is first produced, usually between seven and twelve months of age. It is also accepted that male pups grow bigger and stronger and more assertive than females before reaching puberty. Neutering can also have an impact on behavior—see *The effects of neutering*, p.143.

Looks can deceive
Sex differences in behavior vary from breed to breed. In general, though, males are only slightly more likely to snap at unknown children; and the German shepherd (*above*), perhaps perceived as an aggressive dog, is less likely to do so than a male golden retriever or cocker spaniel. Male Labradors, on the other hand, are less likely to snap at unknown children than the average male dog.

> "I'm all boy, and I'm ready to play."

> "We girls are smarter than you boys."

Typical male
Male dogs are more active than females, demand greater amounts of play, urine-scent more often, tend to be more destructive, and run a higher risk of straying from home.

Typical female
In general, female dogs like their owners to make a fuss over them, and they will actively seek human attention. They are also more companionable than typical males.

"*Please give me some attention.*"

Smaller, rounded head

The female of the species
There can be curious variations in behavior. Breeders report that male toy poodles are more reliable with unknown children than the females.

Female's coat is less dense

Female's body is smaller than male's

Male has larger head and body

More refined limbs

Heavier long bones

Subtle differences
In most breeds, female dogs are easier to obedience-train and housebreak, and they demand more affection from their owners, while male dogs are more likely to be aggressive with other male dogs and act in a dominant manner. Even placid-looking golden retrievers can snap when least expected. There are no appreciable sex differences in watchdog barking, excitability, or playfulness.

Coat color

WHEN FOXES IN SIBERIA were selectively bred, over a period of 45 years, to approach humans fearlessly and nonaggressively, breeders also saw, when choosing for tameness, an unexpected increase in the number of coat colors, particularly black-and-white piebald coats. In dogs, too, there are temperament differences that seem to be associated with coat color. Technically, these temperament changes may be associated with the body's hormone systems—how the pituitary gland at the base of the brain and the adrenal glands beside the kidneys interact with each other. The underlying theme is that black-coated individuals within a breed are more relaxed and reliable than golden-, apricot-, or yellow-coated individuals of the same breed.

Clipped for comfort

Standard poodles
Breeders of standard poodles report that white and brown poodles are more likely to whine for attention than black ones, but apricot poodles whine the most. They also say that black poodles are easier to house-train, more willing to play with other dogs, better at obedience training, and less likely to disobey than apricot poodles.

German shepherd dogs
Black German shepherds are reported to enjoy being petted more and to be more playful and reliable with unknown children than the black-and-tans. Fawn or white ones tend to be more disobedient, nervous, and wary of strangers.

Labrador retrievers
Breeders report that yellow Labradors are more excitable, destructive, and disobedient than black Labradors—and they bark more. Yellow Labradors are also reportedly better house guards than their black littermates.

Dog appears innocent-looking

Predicting coat color

Genetic fingerprinting can be used to predict the coat colors of pups in multicolored litters. For example, by examining cheek swabs from breeding Labradors, it is possible to predict how many pups will be yellow, how many black, and how many brown. By DNA-testing sires and dams, breeders can more accurately select the colors of pups.

Insulating hair protects limbs

Cocker spaniels

Some cocker spaniels have what vets describe as "avalanche of rage" syndrome. A "rage" cocker spaniel suddenly and aggressively turns on its owners and then, just as abruptly, returns to its natural, easy-going demeanor. While owners report that this is not uncommon in golden cocker spaniels, this rather undesirable trait is almost never reported in particolored (black-and-white) individuals.

Social order

JUST LIKE US, dogs have a structured social order consisting of top dogs, challengers, dogs content with their position, and underdogs. Maintaining a pecking order or hierarchy within the group is vital if fights to the death within the pack are to be avoided. The hierarchy is established through often subtle ritual displays that reveal the mental and physical strengths and weaknesses of the participants. Although greater size helps, it is not necessary for these displays. Confident small dogs can be very adept at signaling to larger ones that they have natural high rank. Once dogs have learned their rank, most are content to behave within the bounds of that position.

Being the top dog

It is easiest to become and remain the top dog in your canine's eyes if you raise your dog from puppyhood. When a pup moves away from its litter and into your home, you become the "parent," and your dog interprets your actions as it did those of its mother or other dogs. This is where it is easy for us to make mistakes. For example, stroking your dog on the top of its head is seen as an act of authority, as is staring at it or standing over it. These actions are excellent for asserting your top-dog position, but if your buddy is naturally submissive, it will soon feel even more insecure. Some dogs need their self-confidence routinely enhanced.

Eye to eye
Meeting for the first time, a Pyrenean mountain dog and a beagle stare at each other and sniff each other's scent. The dog that maintains eye contact the longest will exert seniority.

"I bet I can outstare you."

"I saw you blink— you lose."

Respect your elders
This golden retriever puppy watches while an older Labrador retriever takes away his toy. The puppy understands that, for the time being, the mature dog has higher rank and can do as he likes.

Eye contact is used to intimidate

"You will do everything I tell you to."

"Please don't hurt me..."

Signs of appeasement
Cowering and pursing her lips, this Dalmatian tells the higher-ranking German shepherd that she offers no challenge.

"I'm small but more confident than you."

Afghan hound moves away from aggressive terrier

Size is not everything
Although much smaller than the Afghan hound, this Yorkshire terrier stands his ground and uses assertive body language to force the larger dog to back away.

The way things are
The stare. The double whammy. Eye-to-eye contact is powerfully important in the social order of dogs and is a simple method for determining relationships from a distance. Both dogs look at each other when they initially meet; the less dominant individual is the first to avert its gaze.

Play activity

DOGS THRIVE ON PLAYFUL ACTIVITY. It is the primary way in which they determine their relationships with each other. Through play, dogs discover one another's strengths and weaknesses. They learn how to manipulate and hone their social skills, and they learn just how far they can go before the invisible line between play and aggression is crossed. Play also acts as an emotional outlet and a way to let off steam. Play activity neutralizes potentially dangerous situations created by dominance disputes and, through ritual, helps dogs to cement their pack relationships. Just like humans, dogs retain an endearingly attractive, lifelong enjoyment of playing. For many, play is an end in itself, carried out simply for the fun of it.

Constructive play

Dogs are always learning, especially during play. They play with us, with each other, or on their own, with practical toys. Safe, chewable toys are ideal for leaving with a dog when you are absent, while fetch toys are excellent both for use in obedience training and for providing your dog with physical exercise and an outlet for pent-up energy. Avoid using fetch toys, however, with dogs that have potential joint problems. Tug-of-war is fun for both of you, but be aware of the implications of the game. If your dog is naturally dominant, it is important that you win and control the toy. If, on the other hand, you have an inherently submissive dog, you will subtly increase its confidence and self-esteem by letting it win at tug-of-war.

1 Scent to investigate
First meetings are always potentially dangerous. These dogs are restrained by their leashes while they scent each other. Neither shows aggression, but the fox terrier is innately superior due to his gender and greater age.

2 Teasing moment
The cocker spaniel rolls over to deflect any possible aggression, but she maintains eye contact to show that she is not merely being cowardly.

3 Playful barking
Sensing there is no danger, and maintaining eye contact, the spaniel bounces up toward the fox terrier's face. This is typical of play behavior.

*Direct eye contact is
constantly maintained*

4 Head to head
Both dogs are now
on equal terms and, using
their forelimbs, box with
each other. They growl, but
like most play activity, the
growl is slightly "theatrical"
and not meant in earnest.

5 Vicious circle
Running in tight circles, the dogs continue
their play behavior. Both try to chew at their
playmate's neck. Very quickly, the dogs have
learned about each other's strong and weak points.

*Dog stands to play from
position of strength*

Dominance

WITHIN ANY GROUP there is always a natural leader, a dominant individual. The successful coordination of a pack's activities depends on that leader's exerting authority over the group. In the great majority of cases, the dominant dog is often a male. He asserts his leadership through displays of dominance—ritualized activities that tell other dogs that a top dog is present. Although always helpful, size is not the most important factor in determining who will be top dog. While Dobermans and Rottweilers are naturally dominant large breeds, many smaller breeds, especially terriers and dachshunds, are often more dominant than breeds several times their size.

Size can be deceiving

Some families choose small dogs because they feel they are easiest to manage. Not so. Small dogs are adept at becoming top dogs through two diametrically extreme routes. Some—Jack Russells come to mind—do so through natural dominance and authority; others scramble to the top of the pecking order by feigning helplessness. They browbeat their owners into carrying them, feeding them only the tastiest food, and never leaving them alone. Dogs can use sophisticated methods to gain power and control.

1 **First sniff**
A male long-haired miniature dachshund makes a dominant investigation of a Pekingese by sniffing her ears and mouth. His tail is raised, and his ears, as erect as they can become, signal the assurance of his actions.

2 **Head-on-neck dominance**
Placing the neck on the other dog's shoulder displays the most common form of dominant body language. Direct eye contact shows the dachshund's confidence.

3 **Last things last**
Having completed his investigation of the front of the Pekingese, the dachshund, still controlling the meeting, turns his attentions to the posterior region of his subject.

"I'll show him who's boss."

1 Confident encounter
Unable to sniff the anal region of the larger dog, a Spinone Italiano, this dachshund scents the prepuce (foreskin) instead. The smaller dog conveys his dominance by taking the lead in these investigations.

2 Problem of size
Having approached the Spinone with great self-confidence, the dachshund has a problem exerting his authority. He is too small to dominate the Spinone physically, but he still actively tries to sniff his mouth.

"Now I can show my status."

3 Exerting authority
When the Spinone eventually lies down, the dachshund can finally show his authority. He sniffs his opponent's head, raises the hair on his back as best he can, and dominantly stares into the eyes of the much larger dog.

Subdominance

ALTHOUGH THERE IS ALWAYS ONE DOG that assumes leadership within a pack, this does not mean that all the other dogs in the pack will behave in a meek and submissive manner. In fact, few dogs behave this way. Most are confident and assertive—although in a less provocative way than the top dog—and are called "subdominant" dogs. The ritual displays when they meet are subtle, often brief, allowing almost instant social interaction. When two subdominant dogs first come together, there is little tension, and the encounter results in either immediate play or relaxed indifference. This is the most common relationship among urban dogs exercised in city parks. It is also the basis of typical meetings between a young pup and an unfamiliar adult dog.

"I'll only put up with this for so long."

Relaxed ears show no threat

Raised tail shows excitement

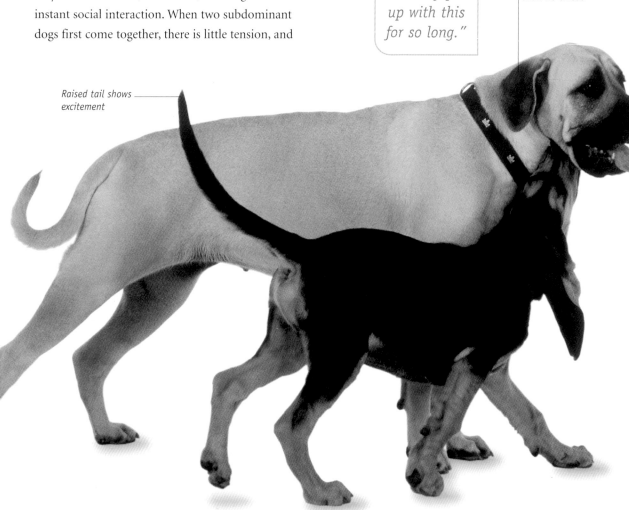

1 Initial encounter
This young bloodhound trots up to a mastiff in an unthreatening way and, forgoing ritual introductions, starts to play. Despite the fact that she knows she is the stronger of the two dogs, the mastiff does not exert her dominance and allows the bloodhound to continue his playful behavior.

"Behave yourself!"

2 Rough play
The younger dog grabs a mouthful of skin and pulls. If the adult mastiff does not repel him, the puppy learns that two dogs can meet and play without having to show overt dominance.

3 Ritual response
The bloodhound exceeds the permitted limits, forcing the mastiff to restrain him by gently pinning him to the ground, using physical force but little threat. The two dogs' shared subdominant status permits harmonious behavior.

"Come on, let's play some more."

"How can you resist me?"

4 Hounded
The bloodhound understands that there has been no overtly dominant threat in the mastiff's behavior. She has behaved subdominantly, as he now does, too, by pawing at her face in an attempt to provoke a further response.

5 Final appeal
The meeting continues with little tension, but by now the mastiff is showing increasing indifference to the bloodhound's provocation. Seeing this, he rolls on his back and continues to demand that she play.

Puppy parties

Dog trainers and veterinarians have long recognized the social advantages of bringing pups together for organized play activity. At a "puppy party" or "puppy kindergarten," young dogs learn social graces, such as how to meet and greet others of their own kind. This form of early socializing is the best route to a measured and socially relaxed adult dog that is content to play and interact with others, whether they are canine or human.

The underdog

MANY, IF NOT MOST, DOG OWNERS feel that their dogs understand their feelings and emotions. This is probably true, because dogs are so adept at understanding body language. Dogs communicate articulately with their bodies, and so do we. We find it easy to understand what dogs are saying to each other (or to us) because so many aspects of our body language are shared. Like dogs, we may show submissive behavior by averting our gaze or dropping our shoulders. This behavior is necessary among dogs if pack members are to follow the commands of their leader and, of course, it is the basis for successfully integrating dogs into our homes. Even the most dominant dog should exhibit routine submissive behavior to the human members of its pack.

Abject submission
By rolling over with his tail between his legs, and his lips and ears back, this Yorkshire terrier shows abject submission. Urinating while cowering is the final stage of submission.

Hangdog
This Weimaraner sits down, hunches his shoulders, and droops his head and ears when he is confronted by a more dominant dog. He averts his eyes to avoid contact.

"I'll obey—just tell me what to do."

Tactical withdrawal
By drawing back his head and lowering his whole body to the floor, a Pekingese defuses an explosive situation when confronted by an equal-sized but dominant dachshund.

Enhancing self-esteem

The ideal house dog is subdominant rather than submissive. A submissive dog's self-worth can be enhanced by avoiding unwitting acts of dominance. When greeting a submissive dog, avoid direct eye contact, crouch down low, and if you stroke it, do so on its chest rather than dominantly on its head or neck. In the most extreme circumstances, the underdog urinates in an act of abject submission. This is also common when young pups get overexcited when greeting people. In both circumstances, move calmly and quietly, totally disregarding the dog. If it is an excitable pup, try to entice it outside and indulge in a little play. If the dog is profoundly submissive, distract it with a food treat to discourage submissive behavior.

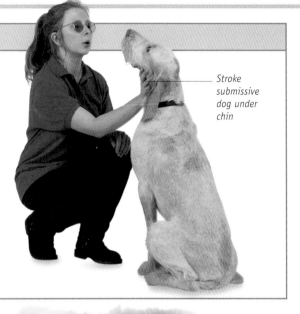

Stroke submissive dog under chin

"I'm no threat to anyone or anything."

Relaxed submission
Many dogs, such as this Shetland sheepdog, submit in a relaxed, contented way when in the presence of the pack leader.

Appeasement gesture
Flattening back his ears, drawing back his lips, and turning his head away, this whippet drops down on his side. He is poised to lift his foreleg in a dramatic show of submission. His tail stays close to his body, where it is out of danger.

Rivalry

"IF YOU HAVE IT, I WANT IT" is a typical dog mantra. Dogs treasure their possessions and frequently want whatever another member of the pack has—just to have it themselves. In these circumstances, only the most dominant of dogs achieve their ends through aggression. For subdominant dogs—that is, the majority of canines—arguing over who gets the object can become a game of deftness and guile. The holder may protect the prize from the other dog's jaws, but if the interloper manages to clamp his teeth on it, the two dogs then enter into a tug-of-war. The prized object may pass back and forth between them, but the eventual winner is often the pack member deemed by both to be subtly more dominant.

1 Jealous onlooker
While a brindle French bulldog chews on a dog toy, his pied littermate watches enviously nearby, taking care not to make overtly dominant and provocative eye contact.

"If you've got it, I want it."

Dog watches patiently while his littermate plays

Toy and food aggression

Some breeds, golden retrievers in particular, can be possessive about their toys and food to the point of aggression. They tend to guard and protect both. If your dog growls when a human or another dog approaches its toys or food, go back to basic training. Offer the dog a food treat in exchange for its toy (as shown here). Reinforce basic obedience and accustom your dog to your presence while he or she eats, including touching the food bowl.

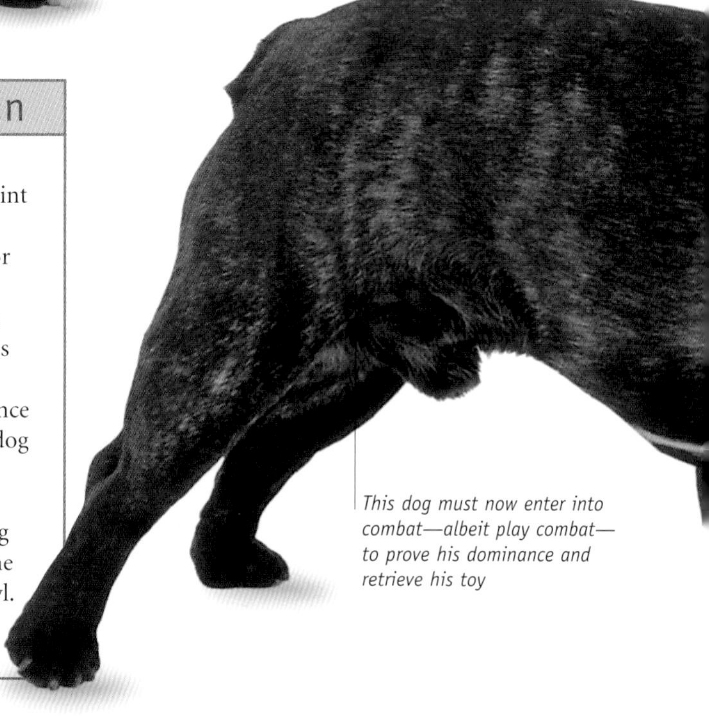

This dog must now enter into combat—albeit play combat—to prove his dominance and retrieve his toy

2 Mock play activity

Because his presence has not provoked aggression, the pied French bulldog now drops into a play position and looks directly at his sibling—and at the dog chew that he desires.

Dog continues to chew, unfazed by imminent attack

Dog drops to lower position ready to make its move

3 Confident grab

Having received no threat through either body language or voice, the pied dog confidently and quickly creeps up and grabs the toy from between the jaws of the other dog.

"No, you can't have it."

4 Protecting the prize

Showing his mild authority, the pied dog now chews on his prize but keeps a wary eye on the brindle dog. This playful rivalry continues as the two dogs repeatedly swap the toy by athletic—and devious—moves.

"You want it? Come and get it!"

Marking territory

IT IS DIFFICULT TO COMPREHEND how sophisticated a dog's sense of smell is. It is the most acute of the dog's senses, capable of detecting odors that even the most advanced technology cannot register. Because odor is so important, dogs use the scent of chemicals in their sweat, urine, and feces to stake out their territories and announce their presence. Urine is the most common territory marker and the bladder an excellent holding tank, always containing a few extra drops for further marking. Feces are voided less frequently, but when a dog does so, it also empties a couple of drops of odor-emitting secretion from its anal sacs, anointing the solid waste with a variety of different forms of information. In fact, almost all bodily discharges—from earwax, to saliva, to sweat—contain odor-emitting information about the producer.

Urine-marking indoors

It is not uncommon for dog owners to mistake the use of urine in territory-marking for a lack of house-training. A canine activity that I frequently see at the veterinary clinic is a perfectly well-trained male dog walking into the examining room and cocking its leg on a table leg. That dog is simply marking its territory. Modifying this behavior requires a different training technique from that used to teach a dog not to urinate indoors.

The female's habits
Female dogs urine-mark their territory less frequently than males, unless they are nearing ovulation. As estrus approaches, the female is likely to drink more and to urinate much more frequently, leaving urine-scent clues telling the ever-receptive males that she is about to ovulate.

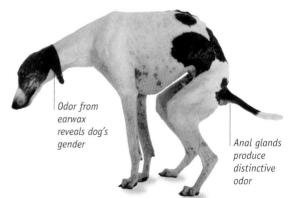

Odor from earwax reveals dog's gender

Anal glands produce distinctive odor

Emitting anal-gland scent
Having emptied his bowels, this greyhound is straining to squeeze his individual scent from his anal glands. This trait is common to both males and females.

1 Marking a scent post
Male dogs, such as this Tervuren (Belgian shepherd dog), cock their legs to urinate on upright objects. Urine marks are intentionally left at the nose level of other dogs. The scent lasts longer on vertical posts than it does on the ground.

"This will let everyone know I was here."

2 Reading scent messages
A male Irish setter passes the same spot and scents the urine. Liquid waste tells him whether the dog who deposited it was male or female. If it was a female, he may be able to tell whether she was ovulating.

"Hmm... Who left this here?"

3 Covering tracks
The setter deposits his own urine to conceal the staler smells of previous visitors. Dogs can mark up to 80 times an hour, and they always have urine in reserve.

"I'll replace that smell with my own."

Defending territory

WHEN DOG OWNERS ARE ASKED why they have a dog, the majority answer, at least in part, that it makes them feel more secure. Regardless of their sex or size, dogs naturally defend what they consider to be either their personal space or their pack's territory. This highly valued behavior can, however, also lead to problems. Sometimes, dogs become territorially aggressive when we do not want them to be—for example, when they are left in cars. There is a strong genetic component to this form of aggression, which is why it is greatest in guard breeds such as German shepherds, Rottweilers, and Doberman pinschers.

Showing teeth indicates aggression

"I'd run away if I were you."

Territorial confidence
At home on his own territory, this Rottweiler cross shows total control. With tail held confidently high and maintaining eye-to-eye contact with the intruder, he barks, bares his teeth, and advances.

"Back off or else!"

Ears are brought forward

Nose wrinkles as lips draw back to reveal teeth

Full threat
With his territory under threat of invasion by a husky, this Doberman barks threats at the intruder. This display constitutes ritual aggression. Dogs usually enter into serious fights only as a last resort.

Territorial aggression

It is in the nature of dogs to defend their own territory. After all, that is one reason that they are so popular: regardless of whether it is true or not, most dog owners feel their companion will protect them. But don't rely on your dog to protect you, your home, and your possessions. By all means, train your dog to bark and growl—that's easy, because it is the natural inclination for many dogs when they hear footsteps. But remember: you are legally responsible for any actions taken by your canine friend. If you are considering any guard-dog training for your pet, seek advice from your vet first.

Mobile territory
In his temporary territory—inside a car—this German shepherd barks aggressively at what he considers to be a threat to his personal space.

Ears are positioned to show dominance

"You don't scare me at all."

Teeth are displayed in show of defiance

Dogged advance
Disregarding the Doberman's threatening behavior, the intruder advances aggressively. By not backing down, the husky has provoked the "home" dog to defend his territory. This is likely to end in a fight.

Chasing

DOGS ARE NATURAL HUNTERS, and they chase instinctively. However, through selective breeding, we have reduced the desire or ability of many individuals to end the chase with a capture and kill. The dog's natural predatory instinct is constructively channeled in some breeds, such as sheepdogs and cattle dogs, allowing them to do part of what comes naturally—stalking—on our behalf. They are trained to slink forward and round up livestock rather than to complete the pursuit with an attack. Without proper training, though, the inherent inclination of many dogs, from the smallest terrier to the seemingly gentlest retriever, is to chase, capture, and bite its prey.

"I'm going to chase him away."

If it moves...
A jogger provokes this dog into giving chase. This can occur in any context, and not just on the dog's own territory. If the jogger suddenly stops and challenges, the dog learns that chasing is not always a rewarding activity.

Predatory aggression

The dog's instinct to chase is triggered by almost any rapid or unexpected movement, from a jogger, a cyclist, a cat, or any other animal. Even the most gentle and reliable of dogs, such as my own female golden retriever, are capable of predatory aggression. Early training is essential to control predatory aggression, but if the habit develops and proves successful, it will be extremely difficult to overcome. Get immediate professional help from either your veterinarian or a skilled dog trainer.

Chasing constructively
Working dogs are trained not to bite, and they express their natural instinct by, for example, creeping up on sheep or cattle. Untrained dogs often revel in the chase and savage their prey.

Cyclists' scourge

The sight of a moving bicycle stimulates this dog to give chase. Because the cyclist continues on his way, rather than stopping to challenge the dog, the canine's predatory and territorial instincts are satisfied. This could form the basis of a habit of chasing cyclists.

"...And don't come back again!"

Head and eyes lowered, ready to stalk prey

"Easy does it... Slowly, slowly..."

Fearful behavior

FEARFUL OR WORRIED BEHAVIOR is most common in dogs that were isolated when young and so have not experienced the advantages of early and varied socialization. It is more common in rural dogs than in urban dogs and more expected in small breeds than in large breeds, although the German shepherd dog is a breed with a high incidence of fearful, worried behavior. Some dogs are frightened by unexpected moving objects—for example, strollers, skateboards, suddenly opened cupboards, or moved chairs. Others react with fright to loud noises, such as thunderstorms or fireworks, while still others develop a fear of hands, either for no reason at all or because of previous negative experiences with other people.

Frown is visible on brow

"I didn't think I was that scary."

Ear position indicates bemusement

Front part of body lowered in submission

Cowering near other dogs
Lack of early socialization of your dog with others can lead to fear of other canines. Fear may result in "preventive aggression" from even the most benign of individuals. Diminish this risk by gently habituating your dog to the presence of others, always making sure to reward calm, nonaggressive behavior.

Fear-induced aggression

Prevent fearful or nervous behavior by exposing a dog during its puppyhood to a variety of social experiences. This is best done with the help and advice of an experienced trainer. If fear of noise develops, this can be overcome by exposing a dog to a recording of that noise (*see below*) and rewarding quiet behavior. Fear of objects is controlled by associating the fearful object with something pleasurable, such as a food treat.

Dog backs away from goat

Sound on CD upsets dog

Fear of noises

Dogs can suddenly develop a fear of common noises, such as thunder or fireworks. CDs of fearful noises are available from dog trainers and vets. Play them, quietly at first, in the presence of your dog until it overcomes its fear.

Wariness of other species

Here, my dog Macy pulls back apprehensively when meeting a goat on a leash. In circumstances such as this, be aware that some dogs may act aggressively, knowing that proactive aggression can be successful in new situations.

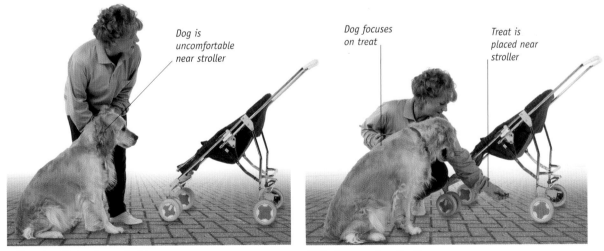

Dog is uncomfortable near stroller

Dog focuses on treat

Treat is placed near stroller

1 Identifying fear of objects

This golden retriever is scared of the inexplicable movement of a stroller. Dogs that live in families with no young children are often afraid of strollers, so they may cower or try to run away if they see one.

2 Overcoming the fear

By placing a tasty food treat on the floor near the stroller, you create an association between the presence of the stroller and a positive experience. This is the basis on which you can reduce your dog's fear of an object.

Fearful gaze
It's a frightening world for some dogs, particularly those that did not experience a full range of social activities as pups. It is natural for us to speak soothingly to a frightened dog, but this rewards its nervous behavior. Command your nervous dog to sit, and then reward a positive response.

Utilizing dogs' abilities

FOR THOUSANDS OF YEARS we have recognized that dogs have abilities more sophisticated than our own. We have, therefore, used dogs to guard, protect, and drive our livestock; to follow scent trails left by game; to point, set, and retrieve; and to guard, attack, or send messages in time of war. More recently, as society has evolved, so have our needs from our dogs. Today, dogs work with humans in new ways—for example, carrying out search and rescue in mountains or after earthquakes and landslides, and working with people with physical disabilities, acting as their eyes or ears. Some well-mannered dogs visit people living in residential care facilities. Other dogs are trained for unexpected uses—for example, sniffing out fungal growth in homes. In each case, we use the dog's natural abilities and, in doing so, we can create challenging and satisfying lives for those with the greatest aptitudes.

Hearing dog
A hearing dog acts as ears for hearing-impaired people. The dog hears the knock at the door, for example, and takes the deaf person to the source of the sound. The dog feels it has been given authority, which can cause dominant breeds such as terriers to feel they are pack leader.

Mountain-rescue dogs
Avalanche and mountain-rescue dogs use their superior ability to follow both ground and air scent to find victims. A trained dog can locate someone buried over a yard deep in snow.

Dog physically helps disabled owner

Acts as eyes for blind owner

Handle for use when out walking

Harness indicates dog is working

Assistance dog
Dogs can be trained to assist people in wheelchairs. They pick up items that have been dropped and turn on light switches. Training is based on the needs of the individual person. Calm dogs, often golden retrievers, are the most successful assistance dogs.

Guide dogs
A guide dog acts as eyes for a blind person. It is trained to help its owner cross roads and to navigate obstacles of risk to the blind owner. Users of guide dogs tend to form very close relationships with their dogs, which offer them an invaluable service.

Earthquake rescue
In the aftermath of disasters, dogs are more successful than any technology at locating people who are trapped. Some are trained to ground-scent to find people trapped by earthquakes or avalanches. Air-scenting is used to track people in forests or mountains.

4 BEING A DOG

Your dog has all the skills of its wild ancestors, but it also has an almost unique skill that is beneficial to both dogs and us. More than any other species, it is socially attuned to humans: our gestures, our voices, and, in a curious way, even our thoughts. Dogs are sensitive to the most subtle changes around them. Using the highly evolved senses of the born predator, they observe us much more acutely than we observe them. They pick up body-language signals that we do not even realize we are sending. For their part, they use their excellent and varied voices to communicate articulately in a variety of ways: howling to call members of the pack, growling in threat or in anger, barking for joy, or whining for attention.

Although not as agile as cats, dogs are still excellent jumpers—and they are far better swimmers. For many, there is no greater pleasure than a paddle in the water.

Canine senses are more sophisticated than ours in many ways. Dogs hear much better than we do. Originally developed to detect the rustling of a rodent on the move, this sense now enables them to home in on the opening of food packaging. And their ability to detect, locate, and identify scents is so refined that it is simply beyond our comprehension.

Just as we find certain scents highly attractive, dogs too find particular odors appealing—so much so that they roll on virtually anything with a pungent or, to us, repellent odor. Decomposing organic material is particularly attractive to the canine nose.

Sight
Vision is important for any dog, but this Border collie uses her sense of sight to keep a vigilant eye on the sheep that she controls in the fields.

Smell
Using his prodigious scenting ability, this beagle sniffs the ground. Dogs can detect some scents diluted to one-millionth of their normal strength.

Hearing
Tilting his head so that sound reaches the ears at fractionally different intervals, this terrier pricks up his ears to focus on a distant noise.

Being scavengers as well as predators, dogs eat and chew a wide variety of foods, paying scant attention to whether they are fresh or not. They chew sticks and bones, for example, and some bury what they regard as excess food, so that it may be dug up when times are hard. Because they are pack animals, dogs are competitive feeders. The dominant dog eats first, and all dogs wolf down their food virtually unchewed to prevent other pack members from eating it—even when you and your family are the only other pack members.

Their sociable gregariousness means that dogs willingly sleep together, although the sleeping positions they assume vary according to breed, age, sex, environmental temperature, and the general level of security that an individual feels. As well as grooming by licking, scratching, and chewing themselves, or by rolling in grass or even dust, some dogs, especially if they are blood relatives, willingly groom each other.

While each individual canine sense is, on its own, well adapted to the needs of a sociable hunter, a single sense is seldom used in isolation. The senses work in harmony. A dog may initially hear another with its ears, then read body language with its eyes, and scent the dog's emotional state with its nose. But it is in its brain, with its well-developed cerebral cortex (the thinking part of the brain) that data is processed before being acted upon.

Taste
Dogs have fewer taste buds than many animals, so it is no wonder that they willingly eat things that you and I would never consider trying.

Voice
A German short-haired pointer raises her head to emit a plaintive howl. She does this in order to call to other members of her pack.

Touch
The sense of touch is vital for grooming. Dogs groom by scratching at their forequarters and chewing and biting at their hindquarters.

Vision

EVEN THE SLIGHTEST OF MOVEMENTS are noticed by dogs. But although they are better than we are at detecting the merest movement at a moderate distance, their close-up vision is not as good as ours. The lenses in a dog's eyes are too large and too rigid to allow for accommodation, which is the adjustment necessary for excellent near vision. In fact, by ten years of age, a dog's sight is quite inefficient. Although not as widely spaced as the wolf's, the dog's eyes are too far apart to give accurate depth of field, and despite having the correct cells in their eyes and brains to see in color, practically speaking they don't use this ability. The main function of your dog's eyes is to notice minimal movement, especially in dim light, and then to concentrate on it intently.

An original gazehound
The Afghan hound is typical of the ancient dog types bred for their acute vision and speed. Its eyes are more sensitive to light and movement than ours are and their slanted positioning gives the breed greater peripheral vision.

Eye care

Through selectively breeding dogs for flat faces, with their accompanying childlike appeal, in breeds such as the Pekingese and pug, we have also unwittingly produced protruding eyes at risk of physical injury. Even when sniffing around in bushes, flat-faced breeds run the risk of bumping into things with their eyes. What complicates this situation is that there appears to be less touch-sensitivity to their eyes, so dogs can damage them without realizing that they are in danger of doing so.

Night vision
This French bulldog can dilate his pupils more than we can, allowing him to take in more light. His eyes also contain more rods, the cells that register low light in black and white.

Slant of eyes lets dog see sideways

"Here's looking at you."

Artificial intelligence
The positioning of this boxer's eyes mimics that seen on a human face. For this reason, she looks like an intelligent dog, whereas dogs with laterally placed eyes are often considered less intelligent-looking.

Natural eyeliner
A husky's eyes are surrounded by dark skin. This was originally intended to help reduce the glare of light as it is reflected from the snow, but it also makes the eyes a prominent feature for communication.

Dog's-eye view 250–290°
Human's-eye view 210°

Seeing things differently
A dog's world differs from ours. We focus on an object, see its color, and decide if it is safe. Frontally placed eyes and many color-sensitive cone cells enable this, though they restrict our angle of vision. For the dog's ancestors, lateral vision was more important than color, which is why dogs' peripheral vision is more acute than ours and their angle of vision is wider (*see above*). While dogs can distinguish between yellow and blue, they see predominantly in shades of gray.

Voice and hearing

ALTHOUGH WOLVES BARK an alarm signal, the dog's bark is more highly evolved, selected by us for its watchdog value. Howling retains its communication purpose and is more highly refined in some breeds than in others, while moaning, whimpering, and whining—all juvenile sounds—are perpetuated in virtually all small dogs, as well as in adults that have developed dependent or close relationships with us. Your dog's hearing is far superior to yours; in fact, the average dog's hearing is four times sharper than that of the average human. Your dog is better at hearing high-pitched noises, too; this is a trait that evolved in its wolf ancestor, whose diet of large herbivores was well supplemented with small animals such as mice, which make high-pitched sounds.

Why bark?
Dogs bark for a variety of reasons. Chiefly, though, barking is used as a threat, a defense warning, a call for attention, a greeting, or a command. It is also very common for dogs to bark while playing.

Head turns to identify and locate distant sounds

"Where did everybody go?"

Plaintive howl
While her partner listens for a reply, a basenji howls plaintively to contact the rest of the pack. Basenjis were never bred for their bark. As a result, they almost never bark, limiting their sounds to a howl or the occasional yip or yelp when frightened or in pain.

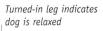

Turned-in leg indicates dog is relaxed

Ruff 'n' roll

This Spinone Italiano howls when he hears doleful songs on the radio. Many dogs howl to music just for the enjoyment of joining in, so the howl is not a complaint: if they disliked the sound, they would simply move away from it.

Dogs localize source of sound by rotating their ears, and brain compares sounds reaching each ear

"Huh? Did someone say 'food'?"

Controlling barking

Barking can be the most offensive canine nuisance when it comes to neighbors. It may be triggered by boredom—by being left at home alone, for example—or by guarding, while responding to perceived danger to you or your home. It is difficult to control this normal activity, and you must understand the reason why your dog is barking before undertaking remedial action. The aim of remedial training is to coach your dog to bark on your command and then to stop when instructed to do so.

Erect ears act as funnel, channeling sounds to eardrum

Hearing prowess

Sounds most easily heard by humans fall within the 1,000–2,000 Hz range, but we can hear up to 20,000 Hz. Dogs hear best at 4,000 Hz but can hear sounds between 15 Hz and 65,000 Hz.

Catching sound waves

This dog quizzically tilts her head to increase her likelihood of locating where a sound is coming from, as we do when confronted with a puzzle. Erect ears are better at capturing sound than lop ears.

Smell

DOGS USE A VARIETY of odors for communication. Urine carries "news" for other dogs to "read," as do feces, anal-gland secretions, and glandular secretions from the lips, feet, and even the dorsal surface of the swishing tail. The dog's use of scent is so sophisticated that we sometimes assume they benefit from a hidden "sixth sense," and indeed they do: the poorly understood vomeronasal organ in the roof of the mouth. Some scientists believe dogs can detect odors at one-millionth of their normal strength. In part, this is because odor molecules are not washed out of the nose with each breath. Instead, they accumulate until there are enough of them for the scent-detecting cells in the nose to detect.

"Yum... You ate something good."

Improving scent
By licking his nose, this chow chow is able to increase the capture of odor molecules. The dog's sense of smell is so powerful due to the fact there are more than 200 million scent-receiving cells in a dog's nose. If the nasal membrane were to be spread out, it would cover an area greater than the dog's body surface.

Ground scenting
A Yorkshire terrier sniffs the ground for scent messages in another dog's urine. Like cats, but unlike us, dogs have a special apparatus in the nose, the vomeronasal organ, that is responsible for the recognition of sex-related odors.

The vomeronasal organ

When a dog licks a substance, the scent chemicals within the substance are transported into the roof of its mouth and to the openings to the vomeronasal organ, which comprises paired chemical scent receptors. Although the vomeronasal organ is known to be directly connected to the brain's limbic system (the part of the brain concerned with emotions), the role of the organ is still poorly understood. What is also known is that it plays an important role in social communication between dogs, because it is the organ that registers messages transmitted by pheromones, which are the body's natural scents.

Frontal sinus

Nasal membranes

Tongue

Vomeronasal organ

Soft palate

Air scenting
This Spinone Italiano searches for odor clues in airborne dust particles and water droplets before lifting her foreleg and "pointing" in the direction of the scent.

"It's coming from that direction!"

"Okay, now—who's the boss here?"

"Don't mind me—I'm just saying hello."

Mutual interrogation
These three basenjis sniff each other to gain information about dominance, sexual status, and pack hierarchy. Because male dogs use their sense of smell to scent out females in season, they make better tracker dogs than bitches.

Friendly investigation
On meeting a new human, dogs will often make their acquaintance in the same way as they would with another dog—that is, with a good sniff. This can sometimes be slightly embarrassing, depending on the human.

Something in the air
The smell of an early morning is both invigorating to us and enticing to dogs. Odor molecules are more pronounced when the air is moist. Dogs are capable of picking up traces of airborne scent and determining which direction the odor is coming from; they can then move in on the source.

Eating

MANUFACTURERS OF DOG FOOD have studied the dog's eating habits and discovered what many dog owners already knew: food preferences develop early in life, and the palatability of a food is not only associated with its taste but also with its smell, its temperature, and its feel in the mouth. Dogs love sweet tastes and, when given the choice, most prefer cooked meat to raw meat. They are also especially fond of cheese and butter. Unlike many other predators, such as cats, dogs are omnivores, eating more than just meat. They have fewer taste buds on their tongues than humans have, so they will gladly consume almost anything that might offer nourishment. This willingness to try anything is combined with a sensitive vomiting reflex, allowing them to reject food that is unpalatable or dangerous.

"I'm really in the mood for some grass."

Side salad
Grass makes a tasty snack. Some dogs are highly selective, searching out and grazing on particular grasses and weeds. Some eat vegetation only when they have stomach upsets.

Hands off
Protecting her food from a human as she would from other members of a canine pack, this springer spaniel turns and growls a warning as she is approached. This is natural canine behavior that humans find socially unacceptable.

"Don't come near me until I'm finished."

Head is held over bowl to prevent intrusion

This defensive stance helps protect food

How much is enough?

All dogs, but especially large and giant breeds, commonly gorge their food. When this characteristic is combined with either boredom or simply increased availability or palatability of what is available, it can lead to the most common canine medical condition: obesity. A lifelong study of 46 Labradors from six litters—all of which lived their lives together, eating the same food, being cared for by the same people—revealed that for those dogs that are fed less and maintain lean physiques, life expectancy is on average 18 months longer than for their siblings that are given 25 percent more food.

Professional beggars
Exemplifying their evolution from hunter to scavenger, these basenjis stand on their hind legs to get near an offered morsel of food. Dogs can be trained to eat almost anything.

"Mmm... nice, cool, fresh water."

Body leans forward

Tongue curls back to lap water

Lapping it up
This boxer dips her tongue into the water and forms it into a cup, throwing the liquid into her mouth. Dogs are often very careful with precious liquids such as milk, not losing a drop, but are much sloppier with water.

Chewing

DOGS ARE NATURAL ROOTERS, chewers, and suckers, with rooting and sucking reflexes already developed in newborn pups. Many of their eating behaviors are similar to ours: craving sweet foods, preferring novel foods, and not eating when anxious or worried. Having evolved from pack animals that hunted and ate mammals larger than themselves, virtually all dogs still enjoy a good gnaw on a bone. Their teeth and jaw muscles are adapted for holding, scraping, and crushing, and they use their forepaws with great dexterity to manipulate bones and hold them in position. As a substitute for bones, most dogs willingly chew on similar objects, such as sticks, toys, rawhide, and edible chews.

Bones-and-raw-food diet

A bones-and-raw-food (or BARF) diet consists of uncooked bones, muscle and organ meat, raw eggs, vegetables, fruit, yogurt, cereals, cottage cheese, herbs, enzymes, and other supplements. This kind of home cooking is a sound alternative to commercial dog food, but be aware of the potential risks. Like us, given a choice, dogs prefer cooked to raw food. Raw bones, meat, and eggs, even from the most hygienic slaughterhouse, may be contaminated by dangerous *E. coli* and *Salmonella* bacteria—germs that healthy dogs can potentially transmit to us. Bones massage the gums and scrape the teeth, but I have carried out more emergency operations for damage to the throat, stomach, and intestines caused by swallowed bones than for any other reason. Dogs love to chew, but what they love is not always what's best for them.

Incisors for tearing

Molars for chewing and grinding

Canines for seizing and piercing

Perfect teeth
This bull terrier displays the equipment that is vital to the carnivore. His jaw is elongated to allow plenty of space for teeth of varying sizes and uses.

"This is the tastiest treat ever!"

Paws grasp bone

Getting a grip
With great dexterity, this basenji holds a bone steady between his paws. He tilts his head to use his large molar teeth for gnawing on his treat.

On guard
This dog drops his forequarters to the ground so that he can more readily chew his toy. He keeps his hindquarters raised, in case he has to move quickly to protect his trophy.

A natural toothbrush
This golden retriever holds his object with crossed paws and gnaws at it. Chewing hard objects cleans his teeth and is necessary to maintain healthy teeth and gums.

Powerful head and jaw muscles crush stick

"It's not a bone, but I'll still chew it."

Sticking with it
Chewing is instinctive, and some dogs will chew whatever they can get their paws on. This Bernese mountain dog is chewing a stick. Be aware, though, that sticks, like bones, can cause mouth injuries.

Burying

MEMBERS OF THE CANINE FAMILY—wolves, foxes, jackals, coyotes, and dogs—all share an instinct to cache food, creating a reserve for times of need. Even the best-fed, most contented four-legged member of your family may have an urge to bury bones and dig them up later. In the absence of bones, dogs may bury food such as bone-shaped biscuits, and some will try digging in the carpet if no soil is available. (I know one Labrador that, in the absence of bones, buries cans of dog food in his back yard, although he leaves it to his owners to dig them up!) Dogs are efficient earth-movers and will also dig to flush out small animals that have gone to ground, to escape confinement, or simply to create a cool patch to lie in.

Channeling this activity

While digging and going to ground are behaviors that have been accentuated in small terriers and dachshunds, even retrievers such as my own dog Macy (seen here, upon scenting a rabbit) will dig in the earth, searching for buried treasure. If your dog is a natural-born digger, it is best to accept this as part of its personality. Channel the behavior by providing a designated area—a sandbox, for example—where it is okay to dig.

> "I'm sure I can smell something."

1 Scent marks the spot
Although it is more than a month since she buried her bone here, this dog finds the site through scent. The smell of the bone percolates through the ground.

> "There's something down here."

2 Getting warmer
The smell of the bone intensifies as the dog digs and she becomes more intent. Some breeds, such as small terriers, were bred to dig out small animals in this way.

"What's that I can feel?"

"I knew it—there's a bone right here."

3 One at a time
When the hole is too deep for digging with both forepaws together, the dog changes technique and scoops out earth with one paw, usually alternating between them. (To fill a hole, forepaws and hind paws are used equally.)

4 Success!
Having found her prize, she reaches in with her mouth and pulls it out. Burying and digging up food provide both mental and physical activity for dogs. Denying them these outlets can lead to unwanted destructive behavior.

5 Enjoying the meal
Having recovered her treasure, the dog settles down for a good gnaw. Dogs willingly chew on the filthiest of finds, but in this instance, the dog's fastidious owner has cleaned the bone.

Marrow is licked from inside bone

"Mmm... it was worth all the effort."

Rolling

NO ONE REALLY KNOWS why dogs roll on disgusting things. Some experts say it is to mask their own scent, to hide their presence from potential prey. Others say they are leaving their own scent on the malodorous material. Whatever the truth, there are other reasons why so many mammals roll on their backs. This is an efficient method by which they rub their heads, necks, backs, and rumps, grooming parts they would otherwise find difficult to reach. Rolling is also a fun activity that releases pent-up energy and is most common when a dog feels contented and safe. Your dog is most likely to roll after it has gotten wet in the rain or after a swim. Some dogs are especially fond of carrying out these workouts in sand or dry soil.

Odor removers

Your dog may enjoy a good roll, but when she comes back smelling of decomposing flesh or other decaying animal matter, it is no fun for you. Shampoos and detergents will eliminate many odors, but some smells are resistant to these substances. Commercially produced sprays are available from veterinary clinics or pet stores to neutralize rather than simply mask unpleasant biological odors.

"Life can't get better than this."

Legs kick up in apparent delight

Pleasure roll
With joyful abandon, this chow chow rolls onto his back, pedaling his legs in the air. At the same time, he arches his back up and down and flips his head from side to side. It seems he does so for the pure pleasure of it.

1 **Catching the scent**
Coming across another animal's droppings, a Spinone Italiano stops to capture the scent in his nose. This is the first sign of premeditated rolling.

"Hmm, that's an intriguing smell!"

2 **Anointing one shoulder**
Rather than joyfully flinging himself on the ground, the Spinone carefully places one shoulder on the substance and rubs it. Some dogs carry out a full roll, then stand up and sniff the substance again before performing a second roll.

"It's going to make a good disguise."

3 **Balancing the smell**
Having covered one shoulder, the dog now methodically places his other shoulder on the animal droppings to make sure that the odor is symmetrically placed on both sides of his body. After completing this stereotypical behavior, he might indulge in a pleasurable roll.

"Excellent! I'll smear it all over..."

Comfort activities

DOGS HAVE DEVELOPED a wide range of behaviors
that are relaxing, conflict-resolving, and often self-
cleaning. Activities such as licking, scratching,
yawning, body-shaking, stretching, back-rubbing, and
wallowing all provide comfort, as well as grooming the
coat and massaging the body. Some dogs groom each
other, which is comforting for both participants. After
resting, being handled, and, most commonly, getting
wet, dogs often vigorously shake their hair back into
position. They also lick their coats and remove any
foreign objects. Some dogs trim their nails by chewing
them and use their dewclaws to clean their ears. Body
openings are meticulously licked clean, especially if
there are discharges from them.

Spit and polish
A supple backbone means that even a large, heavy dog,
such as this Rhodesian ridgeback, can reach around to
lick clean her genital region.

Stimulating the skin
Scratching, as this basset hound is
doing, is a natural way to stimulate
the oil glands of the coat. However,
be aware that excessive
scratching suggests
the presence of a
skin irritation.

*"Oooh, yes,
right there.
Aaahhh..."*

"Yum, you taste good."

"I hate feeling wet. Time to spin dry!"

Spin dry

After a bath, this Bouvier des Flandres puppy vigorously shakes the water from his coat. If he did not do this, the water would eventually penetrate through his almost waterproof undercoat.

Mutual grooming

A male Japanese Akita licks the ear and head region of a young cocker spaniel bitch. Licking is usually part of maternal behavior. This type of grooming, however, has distinct sexual associations.

Body shake

Upon awakening, this Weimaraner briskly shakes himself. He starts with his head and creates a wave of motion that moves smoothly down the length of his body, finishing with a flutter of his tail.

Tactile sense

On the skin, there are nerve receptors for touch, pressure, temperature, position, movement, chemical stimulation, and pain. More touch receptors are located at the base of every hair, and especially at the base of the tactile hairs, the vibrissae. Touch is perhaps the most primitive sense. Stroking your dog calms her, lowers her heart rate, and reduces her stress. Giving your dog a deep muscle massage by using long, firm strokes from the head to the hindquarters is the most effective way to relax her.

Sleeping

DOGS NATURALLY SLEEP for short, frequent periods. An active dog sleeps around eight hours each day, although a dog kept indoors sleeps closer to 12 or more hours each day. (Newborn pups sleep for about 23 hours each day.) A dog's sleep–wake cycle can be altered without any noticeable stress—changing time zones just doesn't seem to bother them. Because dogs naturally coordinate their activities to human timetables, your dog is likely to sleep when you do. Dogs also take catnaps, relaxing with their eyes closed, especially when the pack leader relaxes. Most sleeping time is light sleep, from which the dog awakens easily, but 20 percent is deep sleep, and this is when dogs dream.

Crates and other beds

Each dog develops his or her own comfortable sleeping position. Some curl up in a tight coil, while others stretch out flat on their sides; still others feel most content sleeping on their backs. Whatever their sleeping position, all dogs will feel safe and comfortable sleeping in a roomy crate if they were introduced to the crate very early in life and look upon it as a safe sanctuary, not as a prison.

Hot dog
By stretching out his hind legs behind him, this Maltese exposes as much as possible of his body surface to the cool floor. This is a puppy trait that is sometimes retained into adulthood.

Creature comfort
A natural comfort-seeker, this Rhodesian ridgeback has curled up to keep warm in the most comfortable place she can find. Yawning occurs when dogs are completely relaxed, especially just before closing their eyes to sleep, but it can also be a sign of nervousness or apprehension.

Comfort items
In the absence of a human or littermate to lie next to, this Labrador puppy has curled up with a soft toy. The feeling of closeness to another comforts the dog.

Let sleeping dogs lie
Like this Yorkshire terrier, which is dozing next to a human companion, most dogs like to sleep against an object that protects their backs. Dominant dogs, however, avoid contact when sleeping and prefer to lie alone.

"I'm dozing, but I know you're there."

"I'll take care of you; you take care of me."

Activity

A DOG'S NATURAL STAMINA is equal to the endurance of a long-distance runner. While cats are built for short, explosive surges of activity, dogs evolved to maintain the chase, to never give up, to outlast prey. Dogs thrive on physical work extended over protracted periods of time. When left to amble on their own, many trot or canter rather than simply walk. Galloping, however, is reserved for the short bursts of speed needed when chasing, playing, or burning off excess energy. Almost all dog breeds have supple spines that make them reasonably agile in tight spaces. While well-muscled, long-legged breeds like greyhounds show balletic grace when racing, others, especially those with heavy bones or short legs, can appear quite clumsy.

Quick change
An Afghan hound abruptly changes direction as he runs. This nimbleness of foot evolved to follow the zigzag movements of dogs' natural prey, such as rabbits.

Tail is held high

Large joint on shortened bone

Full tilt
Because he is a true dwarf—with a natural-size body but short legs—this basset hound appears clumsy as he gallops. Even so, he can still outrun all but the very fastest humans.

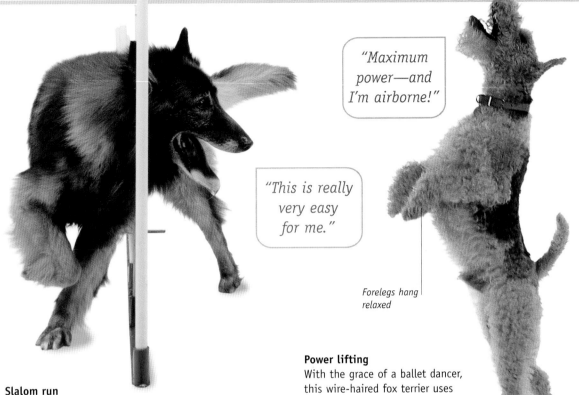

"Maximum power—and I'm airborne!"

"This is really very easy for me."

Forelegs hang relaxed

Power lifting

With the grace of a ballet dancer, this wire-haired fox terrier uses the powerful muscles of his hind legs to leap from the ground. Some dogs can leap up to three times their own height.

Slalom run

A Tervuren (Belgian shepherd dog) weaves through an obstacle course, his agility enhanced by the fact that there is no canine equivalent of the collarbone. This makes the joints between the forelegs and the body very flexible.

"Don't laugh— I'm faster than you."

Regular exercise

It is simple and logical and applies as much to our dogs as it does to us: routine exercise refreshes the mind and the body. But it does more than that. Dogs that have routine physical exercise—which is a natural outlet for their need to use their minds and bodies—are less likely to develop a wide range of behavioral problems, from inappropriate digging, barking, and chewing, to severe manifestations of boredom, such as stereotypical displays of restlessness and pacing.

Agility

PRACTICE MAKES PERFECT, but even so, most dogs are still surprisingly good natural jumpers. All but the heaviest breeds and those with short legs are able to jump several times their own height. Dogs will jump spontaneously when they are suddenly confronted by an obstruction such as a ditch or fence. If they have more time, they eye the obstacle and measure their stride before jumping over it. Almost all dogs want to jump, but this can be a dangerous pursuit for some of them. Giant breeds can actually suffer internal injuries if they land too heavily, and even slightly overweight dogs can tear ligaments in their hind legs. Generally speaking, jumping should be avoided in individuals with inherited forms of joint disease—conditions such as hip or elbow dysplasia.

3 Over the top
Having reached his projected altitude, the dog continues to draw in his hind legs, but now he also starts to extend his front legs.

2 Airborne
Now in the air, the dog starts to draw up his hind legs. At all times he keeps his eyes focused on the object of his attention. Concentrating too hard on jumping might make him miss his objective.

Front legs are tucked tightly into body

"Here we go: up, up, and awaaaay!"

1 Cleared for takeoff
Using his powerful hind-leg muscles, this Rottweiler-cross propels himself off the ground. At the same time, he draws in his front legs to avoid injuring them, creating an ideal aerodynamic shape.

Care for the joints

Selective breeding has increased the incidence of inherited joint disease, especially among some of the world's most popular breeds, such as the German shepherd and the Labrador retriever. This X-ray of arthritic hips shows that the balls at the tops of the long bones (femurs) do not sit deeply in the hip sockets. If your dog is potentially prone to joint disease, make sure you feed it a diet that is high in natural joint nutrients, such as glucosamine and chondroitin sulfate, keep it slim, and avoid playing any games such as Frisbee-catching that involve jumping or landing heavily on either the fore- or hind limbs.

Fashionable athletes
All dogs with well-proportioned bodies have a natural and graceful agility. This bichon frise revels in the exhilaration of using its muscles and joints as they were intended. Small, well-muscled dogs can typically jump three or four times their own height.

"Over the top and now back to earth."

4 Starting descent
The dog now uses his tail more, curling it forward to assist his balance. He continues to focus his attention on his target as he comes down.

Legs are held almost straight during descent

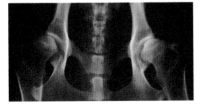

Normal hip joints

Arthritic hip joints

5 Coming in to land
The dog's front legs reach down with flat paws for landing. The hind legs are still extended, having been raised high to prevent injuries.

Paws reach out for landing

Fun activities
Your dog thrives on physical exercise and has a natural
need to release energy. Help your dog maintain muscle
tone and body condition by training him to respond to
your obedience commands, then letting him fly like the
wind as he exercises mind and body in natural behaviors.

5 LIVING WITH US

Some people feel awkward when they say they "own" a dog. How can you "own" another sentient living being, they argue, when that animal has not had the opportunity to decide whether it wants to be "owned"? So, they say they are their dog's "caretakers" or "stewards" instead. If your dog could talk, though, I am sure she would tell you she does not care what word you use to describe your relationship with her, or hers with you. She would not even mind if you called her a parasite. She feels completely comfortable in a human pack because we share so many social, psychological, and even physiological attributes.

Dogs settle into our lives easily because their body rhythms are similar to ours. They sleep when we do, are active when we are, and learn both their own

and our feeding times to the minute. But there can be problems. For example, without natural outlets for their sex drive, some male dogs transfer their natural needs to any available human leg or sofa cushion.

You are pack leader, so it is your attention that your dog seeks. He relies on you to provide mental and physical stimulation. You feed him, groom him, house him, play with him, and protect him. In return, all of his behaviors evolve around you and your family.

Because we are, or at least should be, "top dogs," we are responsible for channeling and controlling our dogs' behavior, for training them to obey commands. But what dogs learn from us always remains only part of the knowledge they acquire. Throughout life, dogs are always observing the world, teaching

Pack leader
Your dog will look to you, as pack leader, for mental stimulation, opportunities for play, and other activities. It is your job as dog owner to provide these essentials.

themselves, and then acting upon what they have learned. Some dogs naturally are jealous if their pack leader—you—shows affection to another dog or even another human. Others become possessive over their food or toys and may threaten not only other dogs but also members of their human family if they come near. As they age, many dogs become more dependent upon their owners. Routine becomes ritual, and any change in routine worries them.

Interestingly, dogs have more active facial muscles than any animals other than primates, and many of their facial expressions are similar to ours. That is probably why we find it easy to understand when they are happy or sad, alert or bored—although it is still possible to misinterpret their actions. Dogs can be destructive when agitated, excited, or worried. We sometimes think this behavior is willful, but in fact it is usually a simple expression of anxiety.

There is truth in the suggestion that dogs are more successful than any other species at integrating into our lives. They thrive on joint activities with us, share our comforts, and, regardless of how large they are, still look upon us as "parents," wanting to lick our faces. Yes, they prey on our instinctive needs for touch, mental and physical activity, companionship, and our need to be needed, but dogs have these needs too, which is why we have built such a successful relationship with each other.

Home comforts
Inevitably, your canine friend will enjoy the comforts of your armchairs, sofas, and beds whenever possible, unless trained by you not to do so.

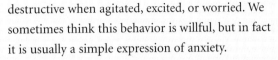

Practicalities
When we take a dog into our home, we need to think about the practical aspects of the situation. A dog such as this, for example, needs a good deal of space.

Sharing your home

DOGS ENJOY COMFORT just as much as we do. They thrive when given the opportunity to participate in the natural world—to lie on a lawn and simply observe nature—but adapt perfectly to our homes, rooms, carpets, chairs, stairs, sofas, and even beds. As sociable creatures, they crave our company and integrate themselves into our routines. (My own dog has chosen to lie by my side right now, as I write.) Your home is your dog's personal territory, and your family is your dog's social circle—its pack. Inveterate pleasure-seekers, when given the opportunity dogs seek out the most comfortable lifestyle possible. This means, unless you give your dog firm instructions to the contrary, it will soon be sleeping on your bed.

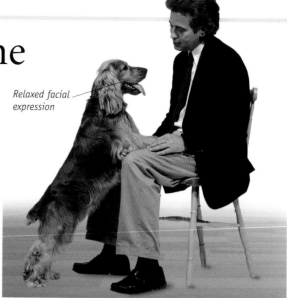

Relaxed facial expression

Greetings
Seeing his pack leader sitting down, this cocker spaniel goes over, stands on his hind legs, and acknowledges his owner's superiority by trying to reach up to his face.

You set the rules

Most dogs aspire to an almost hedonistic existence: by the fireside when it is cold and on the softest bedding whenever relaxing. Your sofas, chairs, and, in particular, beds are not only soft and pleasurable, they also offer the comforting odor of you and your family. Unless you train your dog to do otherwise, expect him to revel in the delights that your furniture provides. If you don't want your dog—and the accompanying muddy paws and hair—on your furniture, ensure that you are consistent with both training and the enforcement of that training.

Be firm, fair, and consistent when training

Freedom of movement
As household pets, most dogs are denied the freedom of going in and out when they please and live in what amount to luxurious prisons. By using a cat-flap as his personal entrance and exit, this Yorkshire terrier can decide when he wants to be indoors or out.

"Inside? Outside? I decide!"

Indoor exercise
A lack of natural outlets for expending energy causes this cocker spaniel to burn up his energy indoors. Your dog may become destructive if it is not given enough exercise.

"It just feels right to carry things."

Chest is pushed out proudly

Daily routine
Bred to fetch, a golden retriever may fulfill this instinct in the home by getting the mail or newspaper. Less conveniently, some dogs may also do the same with your shoes or slippers.

Scavenging

YOUR DOG is an opportunistic eater. If he chances upon something edible, he will quickly eat it. He is also a natural scrounger and an inquisitive scavenger. He will take food wherever and whenever he finds it. Scavenging is doubly rewarding because it satisfies both your dog's need to hunt and his constant desire to snack, eat, and drink frequently. Because dogs have far fewer taste buds than many other animals, they are willing to eat virtually whatever is at hand—from discarded fast food, to decomposing meat, to the droppings of other animals. This is a common—and, to us, particularly disgusting—habit, most frequently seen in large breeds such as Labradors. "Stealing" food is perfectly natural canine behavior, which is why it can be so difficult to train dogs not to scavenge. Your dog doesn't think he's stealing—he is "discovering."

Uninvited guest
Not having been taught that it is antisocial behavior in human terms, a Briard naturally—and innocently—stands up to eat a meal straight off the dinner plate she has found.

Domestic rubbish
By leaving bags of garbage around the kitchen, you are unwittingly encouraging scavenging. This golden retriever has found something tasty inside one of the bags.

Simple prevention

It is always easier to avoid or prevent problems than it is to overcome them, especially when the problem is, from the dog's perspective, a perfectly natural activity. Deter scavenging at home by ensuring that all garbage is kept in securely covered containers and no food is left out within your dog's reach. If your dog is an inveterate outdoor scavenger, simply fit him with a comfortable muzzle that permits vigorous exercise and drinking but prevents eating.

Well-fitted muzzle allows drinking and easy breathing

"Yippee— it's carry-out day!"

Discarded food
This beagle is feasting on the remains of carry-out food in the street. Discourage this kind of behavior by pulling your dog away from its discovered treasure.

Drink problem
After checking that no one is around, a Weimaraner takes the opportunity to lap up tea from a mug left on the floor. Most dogs will risk trying the taste of almost anything.

"Your trash is my next snack."

Meeting other animals

WHILE THE DOG is a natural carnivore, likely
to chase anything that moves quickly, it is also
naturally sociable and open to cordial, often amusing
encounters with virtually all other species. Indeed,
one of the dog's primary inherent attributes, one of
the cardinal reasons that the dog fits into our lives
so well, is its ability to get along with other species. In
some circumstances—for example, in its relationship
with a family cat—the dog will consider another
animal part of its extended family, often higher in
the pecking order than itself. In other situations—
for example, in its relationship with farm animals—
the dog simply controls its predatory instincts.
Selective breeding has reduced the dog's natural
predatory behavior, but it has not extinguished
its curiosity about other living beings.

Control early experiences

Virtually any dog of any age can be trained to
show neither predatory aggression nor fear when
in the presence of other animals. However, training
is easiest, fastest, and most natural when a dog is
young—ideally less than three months old. Plan
ahead. If you can, ask the breeder to ensure that the
pups meet other species under safe circumstances.
By continuing with these encounters—with cats,
other dogs, horses, livestock, and even wildlife—
while your pup is still young, you will reduce the
likelihood of future behavior problems.

Early encounter
A young puppy examines a kitten, which
confidently holds its ground. By
meeting cats now, this pup is less
likely to chase them later in life.

"You're
just like my
littermates."

Position of
ears indicates
interest

Leg is raised
as puppy starts
to withdraw

"I've never seen a dog like you before."

Follow that tortoise
A Yorkshire terrier follows a tortoise across the floor. This dog's boundless curiosity induces her to investigate anything that moves.

Dangerous moment
The sight of a pet rat triggers the Shar-Pei's interest. The dog might simply investigate, or he might pounce open-jawed. Take great care when introducing dogs to small pets.

"Just look at you—you're huge!"

Dog sits to ponder pony

Sizing it up
With some trepidation, this Weimaraner sits and stares at the pony. Fear can be stimulated by a meeting with such a large animal, with unpredictable results. Meetings should always be supervised.

Making acquaintances

Dogs are as capable as we are of forming relationships with other species. Of course they readily do so with us, but they can also form friendships with potential prey, such as cats, if they meet them under controlled circumstances. Almost invariably, the cat becomes the dominant partner.

Fight or flight

JUST LIKE US, when confronted by what is considered dangerous, dogs show their fear in one of three ways. Their first reaction is to stop, back off, and, if necessary, flee or at least hide. If this is not possible, there are two other choices: to fight or, through body language, attempt to defuse the situation by assuming a submissive posture. When worried or concerned, even the most dominant dog can be frightened by strange sights or sounds, larger animals, or anything new and unexpected. Regrettably, I see this a few times each week when dogs visiting my clinic hide in trepidation behind their owners or under chairs. Fear can be learned, but it is also an inherited trait in some breeds, such as pointers and German shepherd dogs.

Leg is lifted submissively

Tower of strength
Dogs feel most secure when their owners are present. They try to hide behind the legs of their "pack leader" when they are worried or feel they are in danger, just as children do. This dog is about to ask to be picked up.

Eye contact is held

"The best defense is attack."

In a corner
With nowhere to hide, this German shepherd dog turns to aggression for security, a common trait of the breed. It is not uncommon for a shivering, fearful dog, with ears back and tail between its legs, to threaten suddenly if it feels cornered.

Fear-induced aggression

A worried dog may cower submissively before suddenly launching a preemptive attack. Fear-induced aggression is difficult to overcome without first reducing the dog's fear of the person or other animal that is perceived as the threat. Some dogs have a generalized fear of other dogs. In such circumstances, it is particularly difficult to retrain the dog, and the best way to contain the problem is simply to avoid frightening situations.

Protective furniture
Frightened by her strange surroundings, this boxer hides under a chair, where her body is protected from above. This is the domestic equivalent of a wolf seeking the security of its den. When approached, she might simply freeze. This is intuitive behavior.

Dog gazes in direction of threat

"They can't reach me under here."

Body is in typical cowering position

Seeking attention

IT IS REALLY QUITE UNCOMPLICATED: if your dog is well integrated into your family, if he is obedient, reliable, and trustworthy, he will want to be an active member of his pack and look upon you as a strong pack leader. He doesn't want to sit around mindlessly counting his toes. He wants activity, be it mental or physical, and you are the means by which he satisfies his desires. Using his voice or his body, he will seek your attention. It is not difficult to understand what he is telling you, but beneath the surface there are also hidden rewards for him. Being touched is as soothing and reassuring for dogs as it is for us. Stroking your dog reduces his blood pressure, heart rate, and skin temperature. It calms him. It diminishes worry and anxiety. It makes him feel more secure. Even dominant dogs solicit attention from a strong human leader.

Emotional blackmail
This Chihuahua stands and scratches at his owner's leg to attract attention. Although this action is a sign of submission, it is quite common for dogs such as this to manipulate their owners into picking them up.

Control attention seeking

When a dog seeks attention—by barking, woofing, or whining, or through physical contact with you—in many instances any response from you, even if it is a verbal reprimand, is in itself justification to your dog that the technique works and should be used again. If you want to reduce your dog's attention-seeking behavior, either never respond to her activity or respond by leaving the room for a symbolic 30 seconds, returning with total disregard for her, including no eye contact. She will soon learn that the behavior either does not work or, in fact, makes matters worse.

Double demands
While her owner reads, one of these golden retrievers woofs to attract attention. The other gathers herself as close as possible, hoping to be comforted through touch.

Head is raised to bark or howl

Eye contact
Dogs superbly use the unblinking stare to gain our attention. Some of us are familiar with the "dog at dawn" gambit, in which the dog comes to the side of the bed and stares at you until you become aware of its presence and wake up.

Leg raised as high as possible

"Over here... Hello... Can you see me?"

Soft touch
A Weimaraner raises a forepaw to get attention from its owner. It is from this basic gesture that dogs are trained to "shake hands."

"I really hope she pets me."

"Hey, look, it's me—your best friend."

Dog enjoys body contact

Dog presses herself against chair

Cheek to cheek
Seeking his owner's attention, this Gordon setter puts his face as close as he can to hers. Although elderly, he is mimicking the way he behaved as a puppy with his mother.

Possessiveness

WE ARE ALL FAMILIAR, from watching wildlife documentaries, with how wolves and other pack-hunting carnivores fight and argue over who eats first, at the "head of the table," at the kill. Dogs, too, guard and protect what they consider to be theirs. This is a natural characteristic that still exists in all dogs but, through selective breeding, has been diminished in pack hounds, which are usually fed from group feeding bowls. Surprisingly, it is most often found in some of the gentlest of breeds, including the amenable golden retriever. Dogs are not only possessive of their food; they often behave possessively over prized objects such as toys, preferred sleeping locations, or even the attention of their special people.

Overcoming the problem

It is the natural inclination of any dog to guard and protect its assets, but possessiveness is a form of dominance and should therefore be controlled. If your dog growls when you stand near his food bowl or won't give up his toys, go back to basic obedience training and reinforce your role as leader of the pack. Children are not seen as naturally dominant and are therefore more likely to encounter this form of aggression. Meetings between dogs and children should always be carefully supervised by adults.

"Back off, buddy—the food's mine!"

Eyes look away to show submission

Puppy moves forward confidently

Guarding food
To prevent the loss of any of his food, this German shepherd dog puppy threatens the tan puppy, who submissively backs away. The German shepherd is dominant because of his size and temperament.

"My turn now. Give me the toy."

Retriever issues pursed-mouth command bark

"It's my toy, not yours. Mine!"

1 **The voice of annoyance**
Seeing a Spinone Italiano playing with a toy, this golden retriever barks to demand the toy for herself. However, the Spinone is not about to give up his prized possession.

"I said, GIVE ME THE TOY!"

Head is thrust forward assertively

"Calm down— I don't want to fight over it."

2 **Visual threat**
The retriever threatens the Spinone by baring her teeth. The Spinone responds to this display by dropping the toy and looking at the aggressor.

"Okay, bully— take it and let me be."

Spinone rolls submissively

"That's better. Some respect at last."

3 **Winning possession**
In order to demonstrate submission to the retriever, the Spinone rolls over, leaving the toy unattended. The retriever can now take the toy. These exchanges between friends are ritualized. The threat is theatrical, as is the rolling over. In other circumstances, the threat is real and can lead to bites.

Playing games

FOR DOGS, PLAYING WITH OTHER DOGS is both fun and informative. Tug-of-war is perhaps the most popular "game" dogs play together. For some, it is played for pure enjoyment: when one "wins," he brings the toy back and coaxes the other dog to play again. For others, it is a means of asserting authority: some dogs are jealous of other dogs' possessions and want them for themselves. Usually, the most self-confident dog wins, but it is not uncommon for a dog of higher ranking to intentionally let a dog of lower rank win, simply to prolong the activity. Games between dogs that live together help reinforce their social positions. Your dog also loves it when you find time each day to play. Dogs need routine mental and physical stimulation and activity, several times daily. If your dog is insecure and unsure of himself, let him win; otherwise, make sure you win. This encourages respect and regard from your canine buddy.

Equal and opposite
This golden retriever and Spinone Italiano stand side by side as they each try to get a better grasp on their toy. These dogs are equal in size and confidence. For them, tugging is simply a game; it is not being used to exert authority.

"I bet you can't take it from me."

Leg lifts as dog jumps away

"Well, I'm going to give it my best shot."

Legs braced, ready to pull back

Shaking it up
To provoke a response from her partner, this basenji teasingly takes the toy. The other dog responds by grabbing at it. Specially made dog toys are best for these games.

Final whistle
A growl from the dominant dog tells the other dog that the game is over. What this means in canine terms is that possession of the object is now final.

Hide-and-seek
This mature Gordon setter enjoys pawing his owner when she "hides" from him. Playing hide-and-seek with people or toys stimulates the dog's desire to search and investigate.

"It's no bird, but I'll chase it anyway."

"Oh yeah, I'm singin' the blue-oos!"

Harmonious relationship
Hearing his owner sing, a Basset Griffon Vendéen joins in the chorus. Seemingly frivolous activities such as this serve to strengthen the bond between you and your dog.

Forelegs are used to balance

Ears show alertness

Legs prepared to land softly

Mission almost impossible
These dogs are using their minds, trying to work out how to catch this highly elusive balloon, at the same time as exercising their bodies. But they depend on you to provide the object of the game and to act as referee.

Practical toys

Nylon, fiber, rubber, and plastic tug-of-war toys are the best toys for dogs to play with. More natural items, such as large bones or rawhide, are more likely to induce possessive aggression and turn a game into a battle. Toys should be brought out for special occasions and their numbers kept to a minimum. When you finish playing, collect the toys and put them away. This reinforces, in your dog's mind, that you are the boss; it also enhances the "value" of the toys, making them more exciting the next time they are brought out. This is especially beneficial when you have to leave your dog home alone—left-out toys will help her pass the time.

It's playtime!

We have chosen the dog as our extra-special companion in part because we share a lifelong joy of playing, but also because we both have a continuing need for mental stimulation. When you share your life with a dog, satisfying the needs of each of you can be mutually enjoyable.

Happiness

IT DOESN'T TAKE MUCH on our part to understand when our dogs are happy and at ease with life. They are superb at telling us—through their body language, their facial expressions, and even their moans and groans of contentment. Intuitively, we understand the sparkle in the bright eyes, the wagging tail, and the mobile ears because, although we do not share some of the dog's physical attributes, we share so many of its expressions and emotions that we know when a dog is carefree and relaxed. Unlike us, dogs do not smile. When they pull back their lips in a greeting, they are acting in a subservient manner as they would to a canine pack leader. Occasionally, however, some dogs do learn to mimic a human smile. Dog happiness may accompany excitement and activity. Equally, it can be the consequence of quiet and relaxation.

"Could I be more relaxed?"

Open offer
Wagging his tail and lifting his leg, a golden retriever subserviently exposes his belly and asks to be stroked. Dogs that are happy in a stable relationship with their owners are likely to show this kind of relaxed behavior.

Playful optimism
Dropping down to its elbows while keeping eye contact with its owner, this soft-coated wheaten terrier asks to be played with. Exuberant, happy dogs are those likely to want others to join them in physical activities.

Tail wags with excitement

Back flexes easily

"I'm so happy to see you— let's play!"

Enjoying life

Although happiness is clearly a human definition, there is little doubt that dogs are "happy"—as we understand the term—when life is pleasurable and enjoyable. They are also sad when denied physical activity, mental stimulation, or contact with their human "family" or other dogs. There is a proven link between emotions and health: sadness or depression can lead to poor health in humans, and it is quite likely that the same applies to dogs. It is healthy to be happy.

Relaxed contentment
This pleasure-seeking golden retriever has ensconced himself in the most comfortable place he can find. Dogs need mental stimulation, but they are also happy when they are relaxed and at ease.

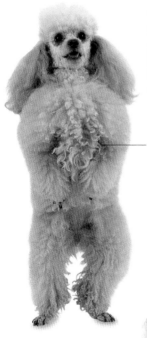

The height of delight
Standing tall, this miniature poodle shows her pleasure by walking on her hind legs. She does this to bring herself closer to her owner's face.

Wrinkling the nose makes the dog sneeze

Forepaws are held in begging position

"Now this is what I call a smile!"

Accomplished mimic
Although he looks fierce, this Dandie Dinmont is simply copying a human smile. This is learned behavior, not inherited from his wolf ancestry.

Joy ride
These bearded collies find it exciting to stick their heads out of the car window. Although this is a potentially dangerous habit, most dogs enjoy it because the sensation of wind on their faces recreates the feel of a high-speed chase.

Excitement

DOGS DO NOT HIDE THEIR EMOTIONS—they are honest. If your dog is glad to see you, he says so with exuberance and joy. But excitement can also be a manifestation of boredom or a lack of suitable outlets for natural behavior such as sexual activity. The tendency to be excitable is partly inherited and partly learned. It is, after all, a characteristic that has been intentionally enhanced in some breeds and diminished in others. For example, small terriers tend to be markedly excitable, while scent hounds such as bassets and bloodhounds are much less so. Excitement is self-satisfying—it acts as its own reward—which is one reason why dogs easily learn to behave this way.

The long goodbye
Seeing his owner about to depart, this cocker spaniel growls and snaps at his pants. The dog feels he can dictate what his owner does, and he becomes recklessly excitable when he anticipates an unwanted departure.

Looking for love
Overexcited by seeing his owner, this golden retriever grabs his leg and uses it as a sex object. Dogs may also behave this way when excited by the arrival of strangers in their homes.

"I'm so happy to see you again!"

Body stretches to reach face

"Not very sexy, but it's all I've got."

Powerful greeting
This Leonberger jumps up to greet his owner, just as he did as a puppy when greeting his mother. Many dogs become overexcited when they see their "leaders," which can be dangerous with a dog as massive as this.

"What?
I'm just saying
hello..."

The effects of neutering

You cannot diminish excitement by neutering your dog. Nor does neutering greatly ease the task of obedience training. However, it is likely to reduce aggression toward other male dogs, simulated sex activity, urine-marking, and "vagrancy" (wandering off on the trail of female scent). Early neutering of a female will perpetuate her youthful personality if it has not already been influenced by female hormone. It also prolongs her life expectancy by, on average, 18 months.

Dominant
dog grasps
submissive dog

Submissive dog
stays still

Ardent excitement
Excited by the presence of another dog, this Tibetan terrier clasps the miniature schnauzer and indulges in mock sex activity. Although males behave this way to show dominance, both males and females will mount other dogs when overexcited.

Boredom

BOREDOM IS THE BANE of many dogs' lives. The most common problem is being left home alone all day. Dogs don't like being alone: they want to be socially active with you, with other people, or with other dogs. Some bored dogs simply look down and dejected and do nothing more than lie around. Others become destructive. They may dig under fences, burrow in the carpet, or scratch at walls. Many use their voices, howling to communicate with the rest of the tribe or barking out of despair at being left alone. No matter how luxurious our homes may appear to be, being left alone in them can lead to frustration in a dog and, in turn, destruction. Although our lives cannot revolve around our dogs' needs, we must alter our routines to ensure the least upset for a dog left at home. By exercising and feeding your dog before you set off for the day, you increase its chances of sleeping and therefore reduce the likelihood of boredom.

"Can we do something fun soon?"

Abject boredom
With nothing better to do, this Hungarian vizsla climbs onto a chair, yawns, looks glum, and shuts her eyes. Her brain and temper will benefit from mental stimulation.

"Someone? Anyone? Just talk to me."

Head is held flat on floor

"Hey, where did every-body go?"

Solitary confinement
In the absence of more constructive activities, this golden retriever shreds a newspaper. If he feels unhappy at being left alone, he may start licking his forepaws obsessively—to the extent that medical attention may be required.

"Can I have a turn with that?"

Something to do
This cocker spaniel gnaws on a chew while his partner looks on. Rubbing your hands on dog toys increases their chance of being chewed in your absence, instead of your furniture.

Distress call
Certain breeds, such as this Doberman, are more prone to separation anxiety than others and howl plaintively when they feel "deserted." Barking—especially continuous, rhythmic barking— is one of the most common manifestations of the frustration dogs feel at being left alone.

An unnatural environment

Good food, a warm environment, and a soft bed may seem the ultimate in luxuries for many dogs. But for inquisitive, mentally alert dogs, such an environment is bland and lacks stimulation. In these circumstances, some bored dogs just relax and chill out, but others create mayhem. Through observation, you can determine whether your dog needs mental activity when he is at home. But there are other things you can do, too—for example:

• Avoid letting your dog become overdependent on you. Dependent dogs are more likely to vocalize if left alone.

• When leaving, do so quietly and unobtrusively. Return in a similar fashion. Your aim should be to avoid turning departures and returns into significant events.

Mental torpor
This sad-looking golden retriever is content simply to watch the world go by. He is resting because he is cut off from the moment-to-moment stimulation that he would find outdoors.

Avoiding boredom

There certainly are advantages for dogs in living with us, but one of the most underestimated disadvantages is boredom. Reduce your dog's level of boredom by setting aside daily "dog time," and be sure to provide practical, interesting toys or activities when you are absent.

Modern uses

THE ROLES OF DOGS have probably changed faster in the last hundred years than in any other period in history. In my grandparents' generation, most dogs still had work to do. They had functional or utilitarian roles: guarding, herding, ratting, protecting. Life may have been difficult, nutrition worse, and disease and injury more common, but dogs were permitted to do what they had evolved to do—constantly use their mental, physical, and sensory capabilities. Today, the overwhelming majority of dogs in North America, Europe, and Japan are kept solely for companionship. We value them primarily for the social and psychological benefits they bring us. Most of us try to ensure that our canine companions lead safe and interesting lives, but if they could talk to us, I am sure that most of them would ask for just a little bit more mental and physical stimulation than we seem able to provide them.

Dogs make a family
A few generations ago, it was normal for three generations of a family to live near each other, sometimes under the same roof. Today, though, large numbers of people live alone, and so the modern dog plays a unique role in providing an outlet for our lifelong need to nurture.

"She seems so pleased to see me."

Dog walks toward welcoming arms

Head bowed for a tickle

Dogs make us smile
Every dog-owner survey reveals the same conclusion: one of the paramount values of living with a dog is the joy it brings to its family. Dogs make us smile. Dogs make us laugh. We feel better for seeing a dog play, eat, and even sleep. Dogs offer light entertainment—a successful adaptation on their part—that is guaranteed to secure their future.

Dog is trained to bite only on command

Dogs protect us

A dog that is well integrated into a human family considers us part of its pack and will act as a sentinel, warning us of potential threats. But while that may mean you are safe from intruders, be aware that if you fall in a lake, your dog is more likely to join you for a swim than save you.

Dogs find new roles

Those dogs lucky enough to have been selected for their therapeutic values thrive as hearing dogs for deaf people, guide dogs for blind people, or assistance dogs for disabled people restricted to wheelchairs. These dogs are ensured lifelong mental and physical activity.

Dogs are a hobby

Through breed, obedience, agility, and countless other canine clubs, millions of individuals use their dog as a focus of leisure activity. You may think that a dog show is nothing more than a pointless beauty contest, but dogs love to show off, meet other dogs and people, and have a stimulating break from the daily routine.

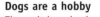

"Nice of them to come along too."

Old age

DOGS MAY AGE PHYSICALLY, but if they could talk, they would tell you they still want to do all those things they have always done: investigate unexpected objects or new odors that have appeared since their last venture outdoors, chew on an interesting toy, and explore new locations. They still even feel jealous when they see you with another dog. Throughout their lives, dogs maintain the capacity to learn. They learn what we teach them, but they also learn from observation and experience. Just as with humans, with advancing years, mental and physical activity may both slow down. The brain actually shrinks in size. But this deterioration can be diminished, even arrested—and the weight of the brain can be increased—by providing routine mental stimulation.

Lifelong training

Old dogs can learn new tricks, but it just takes them a little longer. Some breeds—boxers come instantly to mind—never want to grow up; others slide with quiet dignity into old age. If they live long enough, elderly dogs eventually exhibit a collection of behavioral changes that, in humans, is called senile dementia. Studies in a wide variety of species reveal the same conclusions: the more a dog uses his mental faculties, the longer those faculties work. Your dog will last longer and remain stronger if, throughout his life, you constantly reinforce basic training and always add new, achievable challenges.

Do not disturb
A puppy backs away from his grandmother, who is snarling because she is surprised by his unexpected approach. Old dogs can become very set in their ways, and they should never be suddenly disturbed.

Different nutritional needs
Provide older dogs with more easily digested food, along with additional vitamins and minerals (especially those that act as antioxidants) and balanced essential fatty acids.

Ensuring joint comfort
Joint pain is inevitable if a dog lives long enough, so you must ensure that your dog's bedding and sleeping areas are easily accessible, soft, and comfortable.

As old as you feel
Seeing the basenji playing with a ball, an elderly Gordon
setter ambles over to join in. Dogs will remain curious and
sociable in old age if they lead stimulating lives.

*"Come on—
just one
game..."*

Old dog, new tricks
Although he is clearly quite old, this golden retriever
still finds it enjoyable to play with a new and interesting
object. Through constant daily exercise, he retains a
youthful enjoyment of life.

Breed characteristics

THROUGH SELECTIVE BREEDING, we have enhanced some canine behaviors and diminished others. In general, the most ancient breeds, genetically speaking, are least responsive to training, while those bred for hunting are most trainable. Some breed characteristics are physical ones, consequences of our own personal vanities, rather than representative of a dog's true self. In some countries and for some breeds, ears or tails, or both, are amputated. This is such a common practice that some people think these dogs were born this way. There is no need for these interventions.

Here is an overview of published reports on the inherent levels of excitability, aggression, and trainability in a selection of breeds. These results apply to populations, rather than to specific individuals.

Breeds	Excitability/Activity			Aggression			Trainability		
	high	med	low	high	med	low	high	med	low
Afghan hound			✓		✓				✓
Airedale terrier	✓			✓				✓	
Akita			✓	✓			✓		
Alaskan malamute			✓	✓					✓
American cocker spaniel	✓				✓			✓	
Australian shepherd			✓			✓	✓		
Australian silky terrier	✓			✓				✓	
Basset hound			✓		✓				✓
Beagle	✓				✓				✓
Bearded collie		✓			✓		✓		
Bichon frise	✓				✓		✓		
Bloodhound			✓		✓				✓
Boston terrier	✓				✓				✓
Boxer	✓				✓				✓
Briard		✓			✓			✓	
Brittany spaniel			✓			✓	✓		
Cairn terrier	✓			✓				✓	
Cavalier King Charles spaniel	✓					✓	✓		
Chesapeake Bay retriever			✓			✓	✓		
Chihuahua	✓			✓				✓	
Chow chow		✓		✓					✓
Dachshund	✓			✓					✓
Dalmatian		✓		✓					✓
Doberman		✓		✓			✓		
English bulldog		✓				✓			✓

Breeds	Excitability/Activity			Aggression			Trainability		
	high	med	low	high	med	low	high	med	low
English cocker spaniel		✓			✓		✓		
German shepherd			✓	✓			✓		
German short-haired pointer			✓			✓	✓		
Golden retriever			✓			✓	✓		
Great Dane			✓	✓					✓
Hungarian vizsla			✓			✓	✓		
Irish setter	✓				✓				✓
Jack Russell terrier	✓				✓				✓
Keeshond			✓		✓		✓		
Labrador retriever			✓		✓		✓		
Lhasa apso	✓				✓				✓
Maltese	✓				✓				✓
Miniature and toy poodles	✓				✓		✓		
Miniature schnauzer	✓			✓				✓	
Newfoundland			✓		✓		✓		
Norwegian elkhound			✓		✓			✓	
Old English sheepdog			✓		✓				✓
Pekingese	✓				✓				✓
Pomeranian	✓				✓			✓	
Pug	✓				✓				✓
Pyrenean mountain dog			✓	✓				✓	
Rottweiler			✓	✓			✓		
Rough collie			✓			✓	✓		
Saint Bernard			✓	✓					✓
Samoyed			✓	✓					✓
Scottish terrier	✓			✓				✓	
Shetland sheepdog	✓				✓		✓		
Shih Tzu	✓				✓		✓		
Siberian husky			✓	✓					✓
Springer spaniels	✓				✓		✓		
Staffordshire bull terrier	✓			✓					✓
Standard poodle			✓		✓		✓		
Weimaraner		✓			✓			✓	
Welsh corgis	✓			✓			✓		
West Highland white terrier	✓			✓					✓
Wire-haired fox terrier	✓			✓					✓
Yorkshire terrier	✓				✓			✓	

Assessing your dog's character

EACH DOG IS AN INDIVIDUAL with its own mind.
Dogs have emotions: they feel happy, sad, jealous,
angry, and exhilarated; they experience pain,
humiliation, elation, and joy. Each has its own
personality, influenced by genetics, hormones, early
learning, and the environment in which a dog finds
itself. Looks can sometimes be deceptive—even
the most appealing-looking dog retains, in some
measure, the traits of its wild forebears.

The hangdog
Some dogs retain the size of certain wolf
breeds but have dramatically altered looks.
With his low-set, lopped ears and sad-
looking eyes, this Spinone Italiano appears
unthreatening and easy-going. Visually, he
gives the impression of a sociable and
relaxed personality, but looks can deceive.
Some dogs that look soft and gentle to us
might in fact be dominant individuals.

*Lopped ears
look non-
threatening*

The infant dog
We have created dogs that serve human
emotional needs. Dogs that look and act
like this Boston terrier bring out the
parent in us. Their large, prominent eyes,
together with their flattened faces and
small bodies, elicit a caring response from
many people. However, this little dog's
personality can be quite at odds with the
image that it projects.

*Large size
similar to
that of wolf
ancestors*

*Large eyes
look innocent
and trusting*

*Small body
appears
infantile and
helpless*

Your dog's personality

Many of us enjoy the company of our pet dogs so much that we tend to overlook or brush aside their misdemeanors. It is possible to assess both the positive and the negative aspects of your dog's personality using the following questionnaire. Score each group of questions separately to help you judge exactly how trainable, domineering, sociable, or active your dog is.

To help in a worldwide study of dog behavior, photocopy the completed questionnaire and send it to: Dr. Bruce Fogle, Box DDK, 86 York Street, London W1H 1QS, England; or scan and email to BRBF@aol.com

Check the most appropriate box from 1 to 5 for each of the statements below.	Almost always (1)	Usually (2)	Variably (3)	Rarely (4)	Almost never (5)	Assess your dog's personality by adding up the scores for each section.
1. My dog:						**1. Trainability**
Is poor at learning obedience						A score of 12 or more means that your dog is trainable and easy to control. Excitable dogs find training difficult because they are easily distracted.
Is or was difficult to housebreak						
Is excitable						
2. My dog:						**2. Submission**
Disobeys or even threatens me						Dogs with scores of more than 20 in this section make the best family pets. If the score is under 10, contact your veterinarian or a dog handler for professional advice.
Is dominant toward other dogs						
Barks at sudden noises at home						
Is aggressive to strangers at home						
Is snappy when disturbed						
3. My dog:						**3. Sociability with humans**
Is hostile to people						Scores of more than 16 show the dogs that have best integrated themselves into human society. A low score means that your pet is poorly socialized and is a potential fear-biter.
Will not accept strangers						
Dislikes being petted						
Is likely to snap at children						
4. My dog:						**4. Sociability with other dogs**
Is fearful of other unknown dogs						Dogs that have scores of 12 or more enjoy canine company. These are the animals that would most appreciate living with another dog.
Is tense and nervous						
Will not play with other dogs						
5. My dog:						**5. Activity**
Is destructive						A score of 16 or more means that your dog is relaxed and self-contained. Dogs with low scores need extra physical and mental activity. These are inherited traits over which you have little control.
Barks when anxious or excited						
Whines/demands my attention						
Demands physical activity						
						Total score
• What breed is your dog?						A score of under 40 means that your companion is a potential problem dog. You should contact your veterinarian for professional advice. A total score of more than 70 means you are sharing your home with an angel.
• What color is your dog?						
• How old was your dog when you acquired him/her?						
• How old is your dog now?						
• Is your dog male or female?						
• Has your dog been spayed/neutered?						
• If so, at what age was your dog spayed/neutered?						
• What country do you live in?						

Index

Useful websites

**DOG TRAINING AND
ACTIVITY ASSOCIATIONS**
US and Canada
Association of Pet Dog Trainers
www.apdt.com

National Association of Dog Obedience
Instructors
www.nadoi.org

North American Dog Agility Council
www.nadac.com

North American Flyball Association
www.flyball.org

US Dog Agility Association
www.usdaa.com

UK and Republic of Ireland
Association of Pet Behaviour
Counsellors
www.apbc.org.uk

Association of Pet Dog Trainers
www.apdt.co.uk

DOG WELFARE
The Humane Society of the
United States
www.hsus.org

Dogs Trust (UK)
www.dogstrust.co.uk

VETERINARY ASSOCIATIONS
American Animal Hospital Association
www.healthypet.com

American Veterinary Medical
Association
www.avma.org

Canadian Veterinary Medical Association
www.canadianveterinarians.net

British Small Animal Veterinary
Association
www.bsava.com

Federation of European Companion
Animal Veterinary Associations
www.fecava.org

BREED REGISTRIES
American Kennel Club
www.akc.org

American Rare Breed Association
www.arba.org

Canadian Kennel Club
www.ckc.ca

The Kennel Club
www.the-kennel-club.org.uk

Irish Kennel Club
www.ikc.ie

International Federation Cynologique
Internationale
www.fci.be

Acknowledgments

Author's acknowledgments

Chance took me into veterinary medicine—lucky chance, for 35 years later I still enjoy clinical practice just as much as when I first started in my profession. It's very satisfying to greet, meet, and inspect a fascinating variety of canines each day. The dogs you see in this book are not only attractive dog models, I know them personally. They've been veterinary clinic visitors—patients of mine—and it's gratifying to see them again here. David Ward took terrific photos.

I've previously had the pleasure of working with David and Sylvia Tombesi-Walton and Simon Murrell of Sands Publishing Solutions, and I appreciate their intelligent and sensible approach to editing and design. Thanks, too, to Macy, my golden retriever, for being so photogenic as she indulged in canine activities across North America and Europe.

Publisher's acknowledgments

Dorling Kindersley would like to thank: Roger Smoothy for planning and attending photographic sessions and initial editorial work; Vanessa Hamilton for design assistance; Janos Marffy for airbrushing; Nylabone Ltd for plastic chews and toys; The Company of Animals Ltd for toys; Jenny Berry for help with dogs and photography; and all the owners who brought their dogs along—there are far too many to name individually, but our thanks go out to all.

PICTURE CREDITS

Dorling Kindersley would like to thank the following for their help with images: Louise Thomas for picture research.

Every attempt has been made to identify and contact copyright holders. The publishers will be glad to rectify, in future editions, any omissions or inaccuracies brought to their attention.

Key: t = top; b = bottom; l = left; r = right; c = center.

1 DK Images; 2-3 DK Images: 6-7 Dr. Bruce Fogle; Tracy Morgan; 12-13 DK Images: Dave King; 14 Corbis: Jim Zuckerman; 15 Alamy: Kevin Schafer (cr); DK Images: Jerry Young (cl), (bl); FLPA: Mandal Ranjit (br); 16 Alamy: Marion Bull; 17 Corbis: Burstein Collection (tr); Christie's Images (bl); North Carolina Museum of Art (tl); 18 DK Images: (cr); Dave King (bl); 19 DK Images: Tracy Morgan (bl); Dr. Bruce Fogle (t); 20 Alamy: Pat Bennett (bc); DK Images: (br); 21 Alamy: Douglas Fisher (tr); Corbis: Dale Spartas (br); DK Images: Dave King (tl); (bl); Jerry Young (bc); 22 Corbis: Charles Phillip Cangialosi; 23 DK Images: Dave King (br); Tracy Morgan (bl); 24 DK Images: Jane Burton; 25 DK Images: Jane Burton (r); Tracy Morgan (l); 26-53 DK Images: Jane Burton; 36-37 Alamy: Visual Language / Kathleen Taylor; 40 DK Images (bl); 46-47 Alamy: Bob Torrez; 49 DK Images: Dave King (b); 50 Corbis: George D Lepp (cr); 53 DK Images: Jerry Young (tr); 54 DK Images: Dave King (br); Steve Shott (cl); 55 DK Images: Tim Ridley (br); 56 DK Images: Steve Shott (cl); 60-61 Alamy: Bryan & Cherry Alexander Photography; 62 DK Images: (tr); 63 DK Images: Tracy Morgan (tl); 64 DK Images: Dave King (cr); Tracy Morgan (tr), (bl), (br); 67 DK Images: Jane Burton (c); Tim Ridley (tl); 68-69 Getty: Stone / Ricky John Molloy; 70 DK Images: Tracy Morgan (bl); 72 DK Images: Tim Ridley (bl); 75 DK Images: Tim Ridley (br); 78 DK Images: Tracy Morgan (bl); 80 DK Images (bl); 83 DK Images: Tim Ridley (tl); 84 Dr. Bruce Fogle (bl); 87 Dr. Bruce Fogle (tr); 88-89 Alamy: Thorsten Eckert; 90 Alamy: Tom Kidd (b); Getty: Stone / Kelvin Murray (tr); 91 Alamy: Thorsten Eckert (br); Craig Holmes (tr); DK Images: Andy Crawford (l); 92 DK Images: Jerry Young (bc); Steve Shott (bl); 93 DK Images (br); 94 DK Images: Dave King (bl); 97 DK Images: Tracy Morgan (tr); Steve Shott (br); 100-101 Getty: Reportage / Graeme Robertson; 104 DK Images (bl); 106 Dr. Bruce Fogle (tr); 108 Dr. Bruce Fogle (tr); 115 Dr. Bruce Fogle (br); 118-119 Alamy: imagebroker / Stephanie Krause-Wieczorek; 120 DK Images; 121 DK Images: Tracy Morgan (bl); Tim Ridley (br); 122 DK Images: Tim Ridley (b); 124 DK Images: Tracy Morgan (bl); 125 DK Images: Tim Ridley (tl) (b); 127 DK Images: Jane Burton (tl); 128-129 Getty: Image Bank / John Kelly; 133 DK Images: Mike Dunning (tl); 138-139 Getty: Stone / Gregg Adams; 140 DK Images: Steve Shott (b); 146-147 Alamy: Stock Connection Distribution / Charles Mann; 148 DK Images: Ray Moller (tr); Tim Ridley (b); 149 Alamy: Phototake Inc / Yoav Levy (tr); DK Images: Tay Moller (b); 150 DK Images: (cr), (bl); Tim Ridley (br).

Background photography by Simon Murrell; all other photography by David Ward.